Contending for Faith:
Defining and Defending Hagin's Original Core of the Word of Faith Movement

A Master's Thesis

Submitted in Partial Fulfillment

of the Master of Divinity

School of Divinity

by

Sean Hirschy

Virginia Beach, Virginia

August, 2024

School of Divinity

Regent University

This is to certify that the master's thesis prepared by:

Sean Hirschy

Titled

CONTENDING FOR FAITH: DEFINING AND DEFENDING HAGIN'S ORIGINAL CORE OF THE WORD OF FAITH MOVEMENT

has been approved by his committee as satisfactory completion of the Capstone Experience requirement of the degree of Master of Divinity

Approved By:

Dr. Ewen Butler, Ph.D., Thesis Chair
School of Divinity

Dr. James Flynn, D.Min., Associate Dean of Instruction & Operations
School of Divinity

August 2024

CONTENDING FOR FAITH:
DEFINING AND DEFENDING HAGIN'S ORIGINAL CORE
OF THE WORD OF FAITH MOVEMENT

ABSTRACT

As someone who has grown up and served in the Word
of Faith movement for my entire life and career, I recognize that
there is much confusion and consternation surrounding the
growing influence of the movement. This is often due to the fact
that it does not operate as a formal denomination and, therefore,
lacks authoritative structures to uphold standards of ethics and
doctrines. For this reason, much of the criticism of the movement
tends to revolve around misunderstandings about what the
movement stands for and where its roots can be located. In this
thesis, I attempt to define the doctrinal center of the movement
around the basics of the Word of Faith teaching originally

propagated by its recognized architect and founder, Kenneth E. Hagin, and to demonstrate both biblically and historically that the movement's core is aligned with historically orthodox Christian faith. Though space restricts the subject matter to the essentials of "who you are in Christ" and the essential operation of faith and words, this should serve as an answer to critics, instruction to students, and pruning for the fringe.

CONTENTS

PREFACE

I would like to begin this work by fully disclosing my background. Since the age of five, I have attended and served in Charismatic/Word of Faith churches. My parents got involved with Word of Faith teaching through cassette tapes and books in the late 1970s and sensed a call to be trained for ministry at Rhema Bible Training Center (now "…College") in Broken Arrow, Oklahoma. We lived in the Tulsa area until the middle of my 6th-grade year.

At that point, the Lord led our family to Dubuque, Iowa, to take over a charismatic church that had blossomed out of a bible study group just a few years before. As a newly minted "pastor's kid," I struggled to own my faith until, finally, at a conference for ministers and their families hosted at Rhema in June of 1990, I rededicated my life to Christ.

A year later, at a Fire by Nite summer youth camp near Tulsa, OK, sponsored by Church on the Move (pastored by Willie George), I answered an altar call, and God powerfully called me into the ministry. I was 17 at the time. When the minister prayed for me, God spoke two words to my heart: "Ministry. Rhema."

As a result of God's leading, immediately after high school, I moved to Broken Arrow again and began my own training at RBTC. It was there that I learned to love the Word of God, to pray effectively, and to discern and follow the leading of God's Spirit. I, along with my new friends and hundreds of other fellow students, grew in my confidence, overcame insecurities, and embraced what God could do through my life. It was during that time that I also learned to rely on God as my source of provision, wisdom, joy, and everything else I would ever need. Since I was in the "missions" program my second year, I also learned a good deal about the cost of answering the call of God to go wherever He would send me, as I took up my cross to follow Him.

At the beginning of my second year of studies, I sensed the Lord directing me to move home after graduation and serve in the youth ministry at my dad's church, under his pastoral leadership. It wasn't the exotic foreign field I had envisioned, but it provided me with a safe space to grow in my gifts and impact the lives of the people in the church – especially the young ones.

A couple years into ministry I got ordained, first through our local church and then through Rhema's ministry association: Rhema Ministerial Association International (RMAI). At my ordination, hands were laid upon me (and around 100 others) by Kenneth E. Hagin.

In my 30 years of ministry, I have been involved in Word of Faith churches and ministries, as well as a variety of ecumenical ones. I have maintained fellowship and credentials through RMAI and began to teach at RBTC while we lived in Germany. (My dad continues to pastor that same church in Iowa and has, in recent years, become a regional director with RMAI.) Today, though we currently live in the US, I continue to help RBTC Europe through occasional teaching, instructor training, and strategic development.

Sean Hirschy

Throughout my entire career I have regularly engaged in various forms of local, regional, national, or international networking – both with charismatic/Word of Faith-type groups, and those made up of leaders from other denominations. Through the ecumenical contact with colleagues from other churches and denominations, I have been able to appreciate the depth and breadth of the tradition of the Christian faith and see what we have in common – as well as the things within the Word of Faith movement that others tend to question or look down upon. However, I have never allowed those differences of opinion to stop me from reaching out to fellow brothers and sisters in Christ. Brother Hagin instilled in us that, since we truly are one Church, we can have fellowship with anyone who believes in the redemptive work of Christ and His blood – at least as far as they are interested.

That said, I believe that we have a lot to learn from one another. The Scriptures teach that the Church is a Body made up of many organs (1 Cor. 12), with many different functions, and each organ has something unique to bring to the entire Body of Christ. Through my interaction with my ecumenical colleagues, from among the Assemblies of God, Baptists, Catholics, Episcopalians, Lutherans, Nazarenes, Presbyterians, Methodists, and a host of other groups, I have seen that each movement has been entrusted with divine resources that they can share with the broader Body of Christ.

This also applies to our movement. Once, after I was praying for the teens in our city with youth directors from two other churches (Catholic and Presbyterian), my Presbyterian friend made an interesting comment. He said, "People talk about a difference between 'believing *in* God' and 'believing God.' When you two pray, I can tell that you 'believe God.'" He was noting a difference in how different people approach prayer and appreciating that our faith needs to be living, active, and resolute. And there's a stewardship regarding that kind of faith that I believe our movement can offer as encouragement and pragmatic instruction to the wider Body of Christ.

However, in 45 years of experience with the Word of Faith movement and 30 years of ministry experience with the broader Church, in both the US and Europe, I have recognized that there is a lot of confusion that surrounds the Word of Faith – both inside and outside the movement. I have heard teaching propagated or labeled as "Word of Faith" that is just error being taught by people with supposed Word of Faith roots or connections. I also often hear the teaching of our movement represented in ways that paint a prejudiced caricature of a few extreme examples instead of an overview of what the movement is really all about.

For this reason, I have set out to research the core of the Word of Faith movement, its background and its teaching, to define and defend it to our brothers and sisters in Christ. I have come to echo Horvath's assertion that "what is needed is a tool to communicate with not only our future leaders and pastors, but also a tool to communicate with the rest of the Body of Christ that we as Charismatic/Word of Faith believers are not outside the mainstream of traditional belief."[1]

With this project, I am attempting to provide some perspective, clarification, and maybe even a little correction, for the dialogue surrounding the WOF movement. My desire is to

---

[1] James Alexander Horvath, "Assessing the Need for Systematic Theology in the Curriculum of Charismatic/ Word of Faith Bible Institutes and Colleges." ProQuest Dissertations & Theses, 2002, 121.

show the biblical foundation for the core WOF doctrine to explain it to outsiders and maybe to call insiders to some introspection and fine-tuning. My hope is that this will help facilitate more contact and communion across the Body of Christ, for the edification of all its members.

Sean Hirschy

INTRODUCTION

Scope and Limits of the Study

Each day, well over a billion people on this planet attempt to live out an authentic representation of the teachings of Christ in their daily lives. This is an incredibly challenging undertaking since Jesus never wrote a book on how to live life in the 21st century, let alone how that should look in Tulsa, Oklahoma, Munich, Germany, or Shanghai, China. In fact, Jesus never wrote a book at all. The only authoritative record of his teachings that we possess are those written down for us by his contemporaries. And this creates some difficulties.

The New Testament writings (as well as those in the Old Testament) are all clothed in the fabric of their time, language, and culture. Because of this fact, every contemporary attempt to live in, with, and for Christ must begin with an interpretation of the language and times of Scripture and a reinterpretation or application into the present cultural setting. This means that every present attempt to live for Christ will be a blend of ancient and contemporary, and every generation and context will be required to use some level of creativity, with the help of the Holy Spirit, to find ways of practically living out the Gospel in their world. As Harrison has noted: "religion…is shaped by the particular historical moment."[2]

That said, we must be careful to note that God has set clear limits on our creative license. In Jude 3, we read: "Beloved, although I was very eager to write to you about our common salvation, I found it necessary to write appealing to you to contend for the faith that was once for all delivered to the saints" (*English Standard Version*).

Jude makes it clear that there is but one "faith" that leads to "our common salvation." He also tells us that this faith is not a

---

[2] Milmon Ferdinand Harrison, "'Name It and Claim It!': The Word of Faith Movement, the 'Faith Message', and the Social Construction of Doctrinal Meaning," 2001, 158.

faith subject to change or self-definition. It is the faith "once for all" delivered to the saints. So, though it has come to us in our time and location, we must recognize that it comes to us with a core that is predefined and eternally established. Our attempts at expression must begin with identifying this core – the one authentic Christian faith – and then preserving this core intact as we clothe it with its expression in our cultural context.

As one studies the New Testament, one becomes increasingly aware of how the Gospel message is presented in different ways to different audiences at different times. In Acts 2, we see Peter preaching to Jews on the Day of Pentecost in a way that presupposes their knowledge of their scriptures. Then, in Acts 17, we see Paul take a radically different approach. He addresses the idolatrous Athenians by appealing to them as "very religious" (v.22), while making use of their own customs, logic, and poetry (v.28). Though these two presentations differ greatly in their content and style, Scripture displays them as equally valid expressions of Gospel ministry. And these are not the only varying presentations we see in Scripture. Besides the contrasting examples of Peter and Paul, the obvious inclusion of four different

Gospels in the New Testament canon demonstrates that one truth can be authentically expressed in a variety of ways.

One of the ways the faith has found expression in recent times is through what is often referred to as the modern "Word of Faith" movement, which has exploded in influence over the last several decades. While it has gained numerable adherents around the globe, there have also arisen a variety of critical voices taking issue with the doctrine and practice it espouses.

While some shrink back from any idea or association that invites criticism, we must recognize that scrutiny is an important and healthy part of the Christian experience. As we read earlier, Jude exhorted his readers to "contend for the faith." Since the faith in its authentic form is the only way that leads to salvation, maintaining the purity of its core is crucial, as these truths ensure eternal security for countless souls.

Realizing these high stakes, it becomes clear why we often see so much contention in the Christian Church – though I must also admit that we have not always done a good job of contending for the faith in a spirit of Christian unity or with the motive of assuring salvation for the lost. Too often, we do not even contend for the faith! Instead, we fall prey to our lower nature and contend for our own preferences and traditions instead of the eternal core of the Gospel. Jude, however, exhorts us to contend for what is worth preserving – the original, apostolic faith – which is why I feel the need to clarify how to approach the subject under consideration.

To make a proper and focused assessment, we must bear the realities of time and culture in mind, while being careful to preserve the faith of the apostles that has been handed down through many generations of the faithful. Just as the apostles applied and expressed the faith in different ways as was fitting to the context in which they were ministering, any contemporary movement will attempt to do the same – albeit with varying degrees of effectiveness. For this reason, just as Paul's innovative ministry among the Gentiles was brought into question and verified as a faithful expression of the faith, contemporary ministry innovations can, will, and should face similar scrutiny. As we read in Jude 3, the faith is not a private matter, but is "delivered to the saints" (plural, describing all believers everywhere) for "our common salvation." The Church is a Body where no part exists alone or unto itself. So, as any group attempts to apply the faith to a new context – whether a new country, age group, or time – their application of the faith should be judged for its faithfulness to the previously mentioned eternal core.

That means that the most important standard for judging any movement is its adherence to the core tenets of the faith that the apostles delivered to the Church. The point is not to judge whether the expression of that movement continues the rituals, rhetorical style, or structural forms of other movements (past or present), though certain essential practices of the apostolic age, such as baptism and the Lord's supper, should be appropriately and necessarily continued.

Furthermore, a movement should not be judged based on what makes someone uncomfortable or challenges their preferred paradigm of ministry. Jesus regularly challenged the Pharisees and their status quo, making them mad enough to murder Him. Yet it was not Jesus who was at fault.

Paul's ministry to the Gentiles is another example. The way he allowed the Gentiles to serve Christ apart from the Law generated considerable discomfort and challenged the apostles to think in entirely new ways about the essentials of the faith. It was his courageous and creative applications that created a stir, leading to the famous Jerusalem Council in Acts 15.

At the Jerusalem council, it was determined that the Jewish and Gentile churches looked very different but were equally faithful expressions of the faith. This has served as a landmark ruling in the approach to the cultural expression of the Christian faith and should guide us as we approach our contemporary assessments. As we look at the modern Word of Faith movement, our goal is not to judge the style of the movement compared to others. The focus will not be placed on its practical approaches to ministry. Rather, we will take a look at the core teachings and determine if they faithfully express the core Gospel message, as written in Scripture and faithfully interpreted through the centuries.

As we do so, we must grapple with another issue that the apostles had to address: As the Gospel left the confines of Jerusalem and spread around the world, a multitude of teachers arose who claimed to belong to the movement. However, though these teachers identified themselves as members of the in-group, their teaching did not always align with the faith delivered to the apostles.

Now, some of their teaching was only slightly errant or incomplete, as in the case of Apollos (Acts 18:24-26). Thankfully, with Apollos, his doctrine only needed to be completed. However, there were others whose teaching was in direct opposition to what the apostles were proclaiming. The best example of such a group were the Judaizers, with whom Paul struggled his entire career, a group who were preaching salvation by Law instead of by grace.

Unsurprisingly, since "there is nothing new under the sun" (Ecc. 1:9c), today's movements, including the Word of Faith movement, deal with similar issues. We still see teachers who are associated with the movement but represent its teaching more or less faithfully.

Sometimes, even the best and most visible leaders of a movement fail to faithfully represent the movement's core beliefs – as when Paul had to publicly confront Peter's hypocrisy (Gal. 2:11-14). Movements generally attempt to minimize this kind of dissonance, both from within the leadership and at the fringe, but it seems that it can never be finally eradicated. After all, though

Paul brilliantly argued against the legalists in his time, they are still with us today.

Because this is the case, when we attempt to assess any movement, we will need to define the core teachings of the movement and examine those through the lens of Scripture, rather than looking at everyone claiming to be a part of the movement and inspecting everything they have ever taught. Just as Peter was prone to show his humanity, and his overall influence was salvageable because it was true to the faith, it would be wise for any would-be assessors of Christian orthodoxy to look at the core of a movement's teachings and not use the extremes as examples of the norm.

Now, that is not to say that errant or erroneous doctrine deserves toleration or excuse. Just as Paul was diligent to confront Peter's error, we must remain diligent in confronting error in our time. Wise leaders will do this in the manner and context where it is most appropriate and most advantageous, steeped in prayer and motivated by love. However, we must also use wisdom in not basing overarching judgments on individual failures or diversions, but rather, on the underlying foundation that makes up the core of a movement.

As someone who has grown up in and around the Word of Faith movement my whole life, I have come to realize that there are many divergent opinions and teachings that tend to fall under the umbrella of those who associate themselves with our group. However, I have also come to recognize, by experience and research, that there is a core of Word of Faith doctrine that forms the basis of how we understand Scripture, identify ourselves, and attempt to live out the Gospel – both in our churches and our daily lives.

Thesis Statement

This essential core of the Word of Faith doctrine defines the movement and should be the focus of academic discussion. However, as Perriman notes, "What [the Word of Faith movement] has not done is mount anything like a serious scholarly defense of its teachings."[3] That being the case, I will begin that conversation here, making the case that the core Word of Faith

---

[3] Andrew Perriman, *Faith, Health & Prosperity* (Waynesboro, GA: Paternoster, 2003), 15.

teaching, when properly clarified and presented, is biblically sound and rooted in historical Christian orthodoxy.

SECTION 1: DEFINING THE MOVEMENT

Brief Overview

The modern Word of Faith movement (also known as the Faith Movement, or Word-Faith movement) is a relatively recent religious grouping, taking shape in the United States after World War II.[4] It can be broadly classified as "an offshoot of postwar Pentecostal revivalism."[5] And though those in the Word of Faith movement often describe themselves as Evangelical and/or Pentecostal, "[t]here is a core of doctrinal teaching that makes the word–faith movement distinctive, and identifiable, a core of

---

[4] Harrison, vii.

[5] Perriman, 77.

teaching ...that sets them apart from other Christian traditions."[6] It is from this teaching that the movement gets its name. Based on the key text of Mark 11:22-24, the movement emphasizes speaking words of faith to receive the blessings of God – especially healing/health and finances/prosperity.

The Word of Faith movement is one of various non-denominational expressions of Christianity that have gained steam since the mid-twentieth century, while mainline denominations have been losing ground. Harrison notes that shifts in postwar attitudes in the U.S. and abroad are attributed with aiding these newer movements in their ascendance.[7] Perriman echoes this idea, adding that during the season of American history when the Word of Faith movement was in its infancy, "the pursuit of physical well-being and material prosperity had become a dominant theme in American culture."[8]

---

[6] Robert M. Bowman, Jr., *The Word-Faith Controversy* (Grand Rapids: Baker Books, 2001), 29.

[7] Harrison, 22 & 65.

[8] Perriman, 64.

Now, the Word of Faith is described as a movement, rather than a denomination, because it manifests as a network of mostly independent churches and ministries bound by similar doctrine and practices, rather than formal organizational structures.[9] And it is important to use the word "similar" here, because individual teachers tend to present their own unique ideas, and even individual teachers can sometimes demonstrate inconsistency in their views.[10]

Because of this lack of a unified structure, the exact development, size, and influence of the movement are difficult to define. Maybe for this reason, there "are no comprehensive accounts of the development and spread of the modern Word of Faith movement."[11] However, since the primary agent that binds the movement together is its doctrine, focusing on the key originator and propagator of that doctrine can help us get a sense of the germination and spread of the movement over time.

---

[9] Ibid., 2.

[10] Bowman, 10.

[11] Perriman, 1.

Kenneth Erwin Hagin (1917-2003) is widely regarded as the founder of the modern Word of Faith movement. Through the many avenues utilized by his ministry over a span of more than 60 years, "Hagin has been the most extensive propagator of contemporary faith teaching."[12]

Several critics argue that Hagin owes much of his teaching's substance to other ministers, among whom E.W. Kenyon and John A. Macmillan are most often mentioned.[13] The overall degree of similarity is difficult to dispute, as comparison of their teachings with Hagin's can reveal a considerable degree of overlap. These similarities are often attributed (by both his followers and critics) to the fact that Hagin demonstrated a near photographic memory and was a voracious reader.[14]

Others have gone so far as to accuse Hagin of plagiarism, while his defenders have appealed that Hagin participated in the practice of borrowing and synthesizing that was normative in his

---

[12] Paul L. King, *Only Believe* (Tulsa: Word & Spirit Press, 2008), 65.

[13] D.R. McConnell, *A Different Gospel* (Peabody, MA: Hendrickson Pub., 1988), 83.

[14] Perriman, 72.

movement at the time.[15] DeArteaga makes the case that Hagin was on his own formational journey, but in a similar cultural moment, so when he discovered Kenyon's material, it closely echoed many of his own perspectives.[16] Whatever the case, it should also be noted that Hagin and his ministry responded to these criticisms by retracting, reworking, or completely rewriting works that appeared questionable.[17]

Taking these things into account, though other authors and ministers likely contributed to Hagin's individual doctrinal positions and approaches, his fusion of various existing elements with his own unique perspectives created the foundation of the Word of Faith movement we see today. For this reason, one can confidently assert that Hagin is "the architect of the teaching in its complete and current form."[18]

---

[15] Harrison, 6; DeArteaga, 244.

[16] William L. De Arteaga, *Quenching the Spirit* (Lake Mary, Fla: Creation House, 1992), 245.

[17] Phone call between Pastor Kenneth W. Hagin, Jr. and the author, June 11, 2024, during which he noted that Hagin, Sr.'s book "The Name of Jesus" had been completely rewritten.

[18] Bowman, 8.

Hagin's ministry emphasis on faith (as the term "Word of Faith" implies) grew out of what he described as a specific call from God in 1950 to "teach My people faith."[19] In describing the experience, he often recounted that the Lord had allowed him to have certain experiences that taught him how to effectively exercise his faith, and that he was to share these lessons with the Church. The first and foremost of these faith experiences was when he received a miraculous healing from an incurable blood condition in 1934 at the age of 16.[20] He describes that healing coming through his application of the words of Jesus in Mark 11:22-24.[21] Because they were so critical in his own life, these scriptures would become the keystone text of both his own ministry and the entire movement that it birthed.

> And Jesus answering saith unto them, Have faith in God. For verily I say unto you, That whosoever shall say unto this mountain, Be thou removed, and be thou cast into the

---

[19] Kenneth Hagin Ministries, "History of the Ministry," accessed August 1, 2024, https://www.rhema.org/index.php?option=com_content&view=article&id=9:history-of-the-ministry&Itemid=132&showall=1&limitstart=.

[20] Kenneth E. Hagin, *Bible Faith Study Course, Kindle Edition* (Tulsa: Kenneth Hagin Ministries,1991), Location 119.

[21] Ibid., Location 824.

sea; and shall not doubt in his heart, but shall believe that those things which he saith shall come to pass; he shall have whatsoever he saith. Therefore I say unto you, What things soever ye desire, when ye pray, believe that ye receive them, and ye shall have them. (*King James Version*, Mark 11:22-24)

Hagin shared often that the call to teach faith came in 1950, which was in the first year of his traveling ministry – having left his final pastorate in 1949.[22] Though he describes his early years of faith ministry as a struggle, his ministry soon found a receptive audience and began to grow. In 1966, he began recording his teaching and broadcasting regularly on the radio.[23] Parallel to his use of audio recordings, he also began to author books. These were generally taken from transcriptions of his sermons, which were edited and then released in the form of books, pocket booklets, and study guides.[24] At the time of his death in 2003, it was reported that there were 65 million copies of his 40+ books in circulation.[25]

---

[22] Ibid.

[23] KHM Website, "History of the Ministry" page.

[24] Phone call between Kenneth W. Hagin, Jr. and the author, June 11, 2024.

[25] Ted Olsen, "Weblog: Kenneth Hagin, 'Word of Faith' Preacher, Dies at 86." Christianity Today. September 1, 2003.

Hagin was committed to using every avenue possible to get his message out to the masses. In addition to church meetings, audio recordings, radio, and books, Kenneth Hagin Ministries began publishing a magazine in 1968, titled "The Word of Faith," which at one time had a monthly circulation of over 500,000.[26]

In 1974, Hagin founded Rhema Bible Training Center (now "…College") to prepare other ministers to carry the message around the country and the world.[27] The original architect and overseer of the school was his son, Kenneth W. Hagin, Jr., who has since succeeded Hagin, Sr. at the helm of Kenneth Hagin Ministries. Under Hagin, Jr.'s leadership, RBTC has expanded to 57 countries around the world, boasting over 120,000 graduates, with over 25,000 currently enrolled (as of April 2024).[28]

---

https://www.christianitytoday.com/ct/2003/septemberweb-only/9-22-11.0.html.

[26] Milmon F. Harrison, "Word of Faith Movement," Encyclopedia.com, accessed August 2, 2024, https://www.encyclopedia.com/religion/legal-and-political-magazines/word-faith-movement.

[27] KHM Website, "History of the Ministry" page.

[28] Internal report, in possession of the author.

Hagin's ministry success and development coincided with another major development on the American religious landscape: In the mid-twentieth century, Pentecostal revivalism "began to give way to the new charismatic movement. Kenneth Hagin was one of those who made the transition to this 'less separatistic,' and 'less legalistic' expression of faith."[29] This charismatic movement manifested itself in a renewed hunger for the work of the Holy Spirit and an intense desire for Bible teaching. It impacted many in the mainline churches and outside them, creating appetites for new forms of ministry that Hagin and his colleagues were uniquely positioned to satisfy. Hagin's teaching, in which he regularly references his supernatural experiences with God, connected with a generation dissatisfied with the status quo of American religion. This generation, eager to pursue their own such experiences, pressed in, often by the hundreds and thousands, to learn the precepts he offered.[30]

---

[29] Perriman, 65.

[30] McConnell, 79.

Though Hagin's ministry began in the United States, his teaching quickly spread around the world – first carried in books and media and then proclaimed by those who learned from them, especially Rhema graduates. Through these means, Hagin's ministry has impacted every inhabited continent of the world. The Word of Faith has become especially influential in Africa, where "[t]raditional religion is meant to ensure fertility, abundance, and longevity."[31] The exact influences that led to its spread there are difficult to identify, though the massive crusades of German evangelist Reinhard Bonnke seem to have played a significant role.[32]

Through his various ministry avenues, Hagin, Sr. was able to raise up and influence a host of other ministers. Many of these started ministries that resembled Hagin's, both in doctrine and approach. Possibly the most well-known of these today is Kenneth

---

[31] Perriman, 7.

[32] Ibid., 6.

Copeland (1936-). Perriman notes that Copeland is probably "the most influential figure in the Word of Faith movement" today.[33]

Copeland founded his ministry in 1968, after following the ministries of Oral Roberts and Kenneth E. Hagin. Copeland's website states that the ministry runs "seven ministry offices around the world: United States, Canada, Africa, Asia, Australia, Europe, Ukraine, and Latin America."[34] In 2015, Kenneth Copeland Ministries "launched the Believer's Voice of Victory Network (now: Victory Channel) with 24/7 programming focused on faith, healing, finances, relationships, finding peace and more."[35] Since 1981, KCM has also hosted yearly conferences featuring a variety of popular Word of Faith teachers. In 2018, they opened their own school: Kenneth Copeland Bible College, near Dallas.[36]

---

[33] Perriman, 4.

[34] Kenneth Copeland Ministries, "About Us," accessed August 1, 2024, https://www.kcm.org/about-us-0.

[35] Ibid.

[36] Kenneth Copeland Ministries. "Kenneth Copeland Bible College Coming Fall 2018." July 10, 2017. https://blog.kcm.org/kenneth-copeland-bible-college-coming-fall-2018/.

Though Copeland may be the most well-known of Hagin's followers, there are many teachers today who are influential in the Word of Faith movement – leading television ministries, hosting conferences, and writing books. And while they generally subscribe to the core Word of Faith doctrines set forth by Hagin, it has also been recognized that many of them have views that are "in some respects more radical than Hagin's own teaching."[37] For this reason, "[a]dvocates and sympathizers of the movement have defended its teaching as both Pentecostal and biblical, while still acknowledging that the movement has suffered various excesses."[38]

Since the Word of Faith movement is not a denomination and, therefore, lacks a unified central structure, it has often suffered from a lack of authoritative doctrinal and ethical accountability. Though several ministerial associations within the movement have been established to provide for this (RMAI, etc.), there remains no single, authoritative structure within the

---

[37] Bowman, 84.

[38] Bowman, 10.

movement.[39] This may explain why critics of the movement often present the excesses and extremes as norms, since they can, in some cases, continue unchecked. As King notes, "Practically speaking, I would conclude that if those in the Pentecostal, charismatic, and contemporary faith movements would exercise more discernment and be more self-critical as did some early Pentecostal leaders, they would be criticized less."[40]

The problem is often that those in the Word of Faith movement carry their non-denominationalism to extremes that can manifest as anti-denominational.[41] Possibly because of Hagin's prominent influence, and his emphasis on the centrality of his personal experiences, others who've followed have often elevated their own experience and perspectives, refusing to hear critique that could bring correction and balance. This is especially true when criticism comes from outsiders, who are often perceived as

---

[39] Harrison, 147.

[40] King, 82.

[41] Harrison, 147.

operating on a lower level of revelation or basing their critique on dead, liberalized intellectualism.[42]

Thankfully, as a young movement, the Word of Faith movement is still undergoing development and maturation. As Horvath notes, continual development is a normal part of any movement's growth.[43] So, as that development continues, one would hope that more leaders across the Word of Faith movement would recognize the danger of allowing extremes to continue unchecked and seek out ways to establish further measures of accountability. After all, the New Testament is clear about the need for sound judgment within the Church, speaking of testing deacons before installing them (1 Timothy 3:10) and testing everything – including prophecies – (1 Thess. 5:21), just to name a couple of examples.

Interestingly, Hagin himself recognized the need for correction within the movement and, near the end of his career, attempted to call his colleagues to account regarding extremes

---

[42] Perriman, 32.

[43] Horvath, 52.

related to prosperity teaching and fundraising methods.[44] His exhortation was later published as a book, titled *The Midas Touch*. However, since the influence Hagin could exert was relational and spiritual, rather than official and authoritative, his cautions were largely ignored.

That said, because Hagin is the recognized architect of the movement's doctrinal foundation and attempted during his lifetime to call his colleagues to balance and biblical accountability, the movement is best defined by the original doctrinal core established by Hagin. Examining it more closely should serve as instructive for those looking to understand the movement and, hopefully, as another way of providing much-needed definition and perspective for those wandering into extremes.

Core Doctrines

Defining Area of Focus

As we begin to examine the core doctrine of the Word of Faith movement, it will help to point out that Hagin and Kenyon

---

[44] Referenced now and again by Rhema/KHM leadership at conferences and gatherings.

both had significant Baptist and Pentecostal ties and influences. E.W. Kenyon was ordained a Baptist shortly after he recommitted his life to Christ and identified himself as a Baptist throughout his career.[45] Kenyon also regularly fellowshipped with, and ministered among, Pentecostals, though he had some doctrinal disagreements with them.[46]

Hagin grew up a Methodist, and then was a Baptist for a time after he was healed.[47] After he received the baptism of the Holy Spirit, he served as an Assemblies of God pastor for 12 years before launching his traveling ministry. Owing to this third phase in the evolution of his beliefs, Bowman explains that "Hagin has put the word–faith teaching into an *explicitly* Pentecostal or charismatic context."[48] This context includes (as one could expect) various doctrinal positions related to the work of the Holy Spirit: Subsequence, tongues as initial evidence, the present-day

---

[45] Joe McIntyre, *E.W. Kenyon and His Message of Faith: The True Story* (Bothell, WA: Empowering Grace Ministries, 2010), 79.

[46] Ibid., 166.

[47] Hagin, *Bible Faith…*, Location 7033.

[48] Bowman, 38.

experience of the 1 Cor. 12 charismata, and the Spirit's active leading/working today. (Hagin's more notable works covering this topic are *Tongues: Beyond the Upper Room, Why Tongues,* and *How You Can Be Led by the Spirit of God.*)[49] The influence of the Pentecostals is also seen in the strong focus on healing ministry, though the emphases within the Word of Faith movement differ in some ways from Pentecostals.

Owing to the Baptist and Pentecostal heritage of the Word of Faith movement, especially Hagin's fellowship in those circles, one finds significant doctrinal overlap between the Word of Faith movement and these groups. For example, Hagin admired and learned from the work of P.C. Nelson, whom he often quotes, and whose *Bible Doctrines* book is used every year as a textbook at Hagin's RBTC.[50]

P.C. Nelson (1868–1942) was a minister and scholar, proficient in 25 languages, whose faith journey mirrored Hagin's

---

[49] *Tongues…*is a compilation of his teaching on the subject released posthumously in 2007. *How You…*was originally published in 1978 and gone through several additions. Both books: Faith Library Publications.

[50] Hagin, *Bible Faith…*, 13 different quotes, the first of which is a reference at Location 147.

in some ways. Nelson was a well-known Baptist evangelist, whose experiences of healing and baptism in the Holy Spirit eventually brought him among the Pentecostals, where he was ordained in the Assemblies of God denomination.[51] As evidence of his continued and profound influence in those circles, the Assemblies of God recently renamed their southwestern university "Nelson University" in his honor.[52]

Recognizing that Hagin's doctrine owes much to his Baptist and Pentecostal roots, for the sake of brevity, we will spend little time discussing basic Christian doctrines held in common among these groups. We will focus attention instead on those doctrines and perspectives that are most central and unique to the doctrine of the Word of Faith movement, including the "past tense" of God's word, "who you are in Christ," and the operation of faith, especially through words.

---

[51] Nelson University, "The Life and Legacy of P.C. Nelson," accessed August 3, 2024. https://nelson.edu/pc-nelson-bio/.

[52] Ibid.

God's Exalted Word

As a broadly evangelical movement, the Word of Faith teachers hold a high view regarding the authority of Scripture, based on verbal plenary inspiration.[53] According to this view: "Every word, word form, and word placement found in the Bible's original manuscripts was divinely and intentionally written."[54] Because of this approach to Scripture, Word of Faith adherents agree with those, like classic faith teacher A.B. Simpson, who wrote, "The word of God is for evermore of the standard of his will."[55] However, several commentators on the movement also point out that Word of Faith teachers hold a unique view of Scripture, in which "the Bible is actually a contract between the born-again believer and God."[56]

As someone with a long history in the movement, I would offer that the word "covenant" is a more accurate (and biblical)

---

[53] Loren Hirschy, 1981 RBTC graduate, email to the author.

[54] Got Questions, "What is Verbal Plenary Inspiration," accessed August 1, 2024, https://www.gotquestions.org/verbal-plenary-inspiration.html.

[55] King, 197.

[56] Harrison, 9.

word than "contract." With a covenant relationship in mind, our movement sees the promises of God in the Bible as similar to the vows one makes in a wedding ceremony: They are not just the terms of a business deal. They are binding, but they are also very personal. A good husband's vows are rooted in love, so he means what he says and gives his all to keep his vows. However, though a human in covenant is bound to fail to keep their promise in some way, God is entirely faithful.

The Word of Faith takes God's word as ultimately trustworthy, because, as Hagin states, "The Bible says God has magnified His Word even above His Name."[57] Hagin bases this comment on the words of Psalm 138:2, "…you have exalted above all things your name and your word." However, the footnote, along with a few other translations (KJV, ERV, YLT…) reads "Or *you have exalted your word above all your name.*" Whether one reads it as his name and word being exalted together or his word being exalted above his name, the sense that God and his word are inseparable is clear. In Word of Faith teaching, this

---

[57] Hagin, *Bible Faith…*, Location 3319.

means that, since God cannot fail, his word cannot fail.[58] This explains what Perriman notes: "In Faith teaching the Word is backed up – underwritten, guaranteed – by God himself."[59]

The Kenneth Hagin Ministries website reads:

> "The Bible is the inspired Word of God, the product of holy men of old who spoke and wrote as they were moved by the Holy Spirit. The New Covenant, as recorded in the New Testament, we accept as our infallible guide in matters pertaining to conduct and doctrine (2 Tim. 3:16; 1 Thess. 2:13; 2 Peter 1:21)."[60]

The Word of Faith view regarding the infallibility and ultimate reliability of Scripture explains why Hagin was known to often repeat the mantra: "The Bible says it. I believe it. That settles it." He also quotes Dr. Lillian B. Yeomans: "God delights in his children stepping out over the aching void with nothing underneath their feet but the Word of God."[61] And because he was

---

[58] Ibid., Location 5778.

[59] Perriman, 41.

[60] Kenneth Hagin Ministries, "What We Believe," accessed August 1, 2024, https://www.rhema.org/index.php?option=com_content&view=article&id=5&Itemid=138.

[61] Hagin, *Bible Faith…*, Location 2531.

committed to the absolute primacy of Scripture, he was famous for his responses when someone would ask for his advice: He would immediately (and, at times, almost frustratingly) respond with "What does the WORD say?"

This emphasis on the centrality and authority of Scripture has strongly impacted the approach and verbiage within the movement. Those within the movement tend to call Word of Faith churches "Word churches." This moniker refers to this emphasis on taking Scripture seriously and to the preaching style that mirrors what one finds in Hagin's books. In his writings, one finds scripture after scripture – explained, illustrated, and backed up with other scriptures to prove a point.[62] (As a further testament to the movement's growth and influence, this preaching style can now be found in a variety of churches of other denominations and groups outside the Word of Faith.)[63]

Though critics often accuse teachers in the Word of Faith movement of basing their doctrine on their experiences, dreams,

---

[62] Harrison, 160.

[63] Ibid.

or visions, Perriman notes that the movement's leaders tend to keep their anchor fixed in Scripture: "For a movement that puts so much store by supernaturally revealed knowledge there is at times a remarkable emphasis on the absolute priority of God's word as the basis for the life of Faith."[64] Sitting under Hagin's teaching live, as I was often able to do from 1992-2003, I remember he would frequently insist that we should believe the Bible, even if it contradicted his teaching. Hagin also cautioned against the Scriptures losing their influence, stating, "Our having to encourage believers to believe or have faith is a result of the Word of God's having lost its reality to us."[65] Knowing his reverence for the Bible has given me, as someone who holds him in great esteem, complete assurance in this process, knowing he would expect his followers to assess his teaching without respect for man in the light of Scripture.

---

[64] Perriman, 35.

[65] K.E. Hagin, *Foundations for Faith* (Tulsa: Kenneth Hagin Ministries, 1998), 63.

Possessing the Benefits

Perriman, reporting for the Alliance Commission on Unity and Truth among Evangelicals in the UK, summarizes Word of Faith teaching in the following manner: "The basic premise of Word of Faith teaching is very simple. By virtue of Christ's death, the believer is entitled not only to salvation and the sanctifying indwelling of the Holy Spirit but also to the material benefits of health and prosperity."[66] As Perriman, and many inside and outside the movement point out, the Word of Faith movement agrees with other traditionally evangelical Christian groups regarding basic Christology, soteriology, pneumatology, eschatology, etc. However, where the Word of Faith differentiates itself is often in its approach to the impact of redemption on the present life of the Church. Sherman states it this way: "The Word of Faith movement teaches that in response to faith, God will prosper his people spiritually, physically, emotionally and financially."[67] Harrison explains: "Three basic points form the

---

[66] Perriman, 19.

[67] Bill Sherman, "BRIEF: Weekend conference to critique Word of Faith movement," Tribune Content Agency, July 7, 2012, https://go.openathens.net/redirector/regent.edu?url=https://www.proquest.com

core of the Faith Message. These are: the principle of knowing who you are in Christ; the practice of positive confession (and positive mental attitude); and a worldview that emphasizes material prosperity and physical health as the divine right of every Christian."[68]

In all three statements above, we see a description of the Word of Faith movement as emphasizing God's working in the here and now, in practical areas of life – especially health and finances. For this reason, many outside the movement refer to the teaching of the Word of Faith movement as the *health and wealth Gospel*.[69] Though often meant as derogatory, the moniker speaks to an important reality: While Word of Faith adherents recognize Scripture's emphasis on the exceeding value of the eternal, in agreement with others in the mainstream of Christianity, they also see in Scripture a host of information regarding God's will for this life. In Hagin's teaching on faith, the emphasis and illustrations

---

/wirefeeds/brief-weekend-conference-critique-word-faith/docview/1023910594/se-2?accountid=13479, 1.

[68] Harrison, 8.

[69] Gee, 3.

largely point to three main areas: The Baptism of the Holy Spirit, physical healing, and financial prosperity/provision.[70]

It is the portions of Scripture relating to God's promises for the present that Word of Faith adherents often view as neglected or misunderstood by other parts of the Church.[71] To overcome this perceived neglect, the Word of Faith focuses attention on these areas to help people experience everything that God has in store for them.[72] In this way, the movement sees itself as a complementary or even corrective influence in the broader Body of Christ.

Above, Perriman uses the word "entitled" to express the *status* that the Word of Faith movement attempts to communicate.

---

[70] Hagin, *Bible Faith...*, as one reads through this book, one notices that these three areas are generally the stories that the author uses to describe the efficacy of faith. His other books are also often focused on one of these three areas. Titles include: *Why Tongues?, Tongues: Beyond the Upper Room, God's Medicine, Healing Scriptures, How God Taught me about Prosperity, and The Midas Touch.*

[71] Hagin, *Bible Faith...*, Location 97. Hagin often referenced, not only his own experiences, but those of many others who came to him with difficulties because they had not been properly taught in their denominational churches.

[72] Harrison, 9.

The idea is that, because of what Christ accomplished on the cross, certain things now belong to us.

Sherman uses the words "in response to faith" to point out the *method* that the Word of Faith sees for making these possibilities become reality. Though God has bestowed certain blessings upon the believer, these must be practically attained through the individual's exercise of faith.

Harrison takes this a step further, explaining that the Word of Faith movement is focused on finding out what God has in store for His people and "taking direct, aggressive action" to enter into it.[73] It is this "direct, aggressive action" – an intentional, experimental, and experiential pragmatism – that seems to set the Word of Faith apart from other approaches to Christian living. Perriman agrees, explaining, "it is the methodology of faith that especially characterizes the movement's teaching and practice: How do we get it to work? How do we guarantee results? How do we account for the apparent failures?"[74]

---

[73] Harrison, 171.

[74] Perriman, 43.

This overall pragmatic approach is largely based on the emphasis within the WOF movement (prevalent in the writings of Kenyon on) on the "past tense" of God's word.[75] The "past tense" approach is based on the concept that God, in his infinite foreknowledge, has *already* provided certain things for his people – primarily through Christ's redemptive work. Because these things are already provided, there remains no more question regarding God's will concerning them in the present. His will for us in these areas has been determined. In other words, the present availability of these blessings is now a given because God exercised his sovereign will in the matter at a past point in history. From God's standpoint, the matter is already decided. Therefore, our response remains the only variable in question regarding the fulfillment of his will.

A cornerstone text for this teaching is Ephesians 1. Note the past tense of many of the verbs in this passage:

> 3 Blessed be the God and Father of our Lord Jesus Christ, who *has blessed us* in Christ with every spiritual blessing in the heavenly places, 4 even as *he chose us* in him before the foundation of the world, that we should be holy and blameless before him. In love 5 *he predestined us* for

---

[75] Harrison, 232.

adoption to himself as sons through Jesus Christ, according to the purpose of his will, 6 to the praise of his glorious grace, with which *he has blessed us* in the Beloved. 7 In him we have redemption through his blood, the forgiveness of our trespasses, according to the riches of his grace, 8 which *he lavished upon us*, in all wisdom and insight 9 making known to us the mystery of his will, according to his *purpose, which he set forth* in Christ 10 as a plan for the fullness of time, to unite all things in him, things in heaven and things on earth.

11 In him *we have obtained an inheritance*, having been predestined according to the purpose of him who works all things according to the counsel of his will, 12 so that we who were the first to hope in Christ might be to the praise of his glory. 13 In him you also, *when you heard the word of truth*, the gospel of your salvation, *and believed* in him, were sealed with the promised Holy Spirit, 14 who is the guarantee of our inheritance until we acquire possession of it, to the praise of his glory. (Ephesians 1:3-14, *emphasis added*)

Much of the overall approach of the Word of Faith message roots itself in the sense of this passage, where we read that God "has blessed us" (v.3) and prepared for us "an inheritance" (v.11) From this perspective, Hagin emphasizes that various blessings "belong to us," including healing, long life, speaking in tongues, and prosperity.[76]

---

[76] Hagin, *Bible Faith...*, Locations 432, 3155, 4660, and 3161.

However, the experience of that inheritance is only activated by hearing about it (v.13) and believing it (v.13). So long as a person has not heard about the benefits that God has prepared (including both the eternal and temporal aspects of redemption), that person is unable to respond to God in faith and experience that benefit. So, for the ignorant person, it is as if those blessings had not been provided at all.

For this reason, hearing and believing are critical to the worldview of the Word of Faith movement. It is through hearing that one becomes aware of what God has prepared. It is through believing that one begins to take possession.

Another major textual basis for this paradigm, and key to much of the movement's teaching on faith, is Romans 10. Here Paul describes the universal availability of salvation, but emphasizes that it must be practically communicated, believed, and then acted upon to be received. In verse 3, he describes the Jews as "ignorant of the righteousness of God," causing them to persist in their own works. In verse 13, he says that "everyone who calls on the name of the Lord will be saved." However, he also goes on to explain that they cannot call on the Lord and receive salvation in their state of ignorance. Someone must be sent to preach to them (v.15). He concludes the section with the note that "faith comes from hearing, and hearing through the word of Christ" (v.17). In other words: Only once one has heard the truth and believed it can he or she then respond appropriately and experience the benefits of Christ's redemptive work.

A commonly used illustration, taken from the concepts in the passage above and Ephesians 1, is an inheritance that has been left for an heir.[77] The heir can only possess the inheritance once they have been informed that they are the beneficiary. And, even then, once the executor informs the beneficiary, the beneficiary must believe the authenticity of the information. Only when the heir believes that the inheritance belongs to them will they actively begin to take possession of it. And, finally, it is only when the heir possesses the inheritance that the benefactor's will has been fully carried out.

Obviously, this concept makes the full manifestation of God's will, in some ways, conditional upon a human response.

---

[77] For example, in Hagin's *Bible Faith Study Course* alone, he uses this concept at least a dozen times.

Some argue that this threatens God's sovereignty. For example: McConnell seems appalled that, "In Faith theology, a *personal* loving God does not determine what comes into the believer's life. [Positive Mental Attitude] and positive confession do."[78]

However, King points out that theologians often differentiate between two sides of the will of God.[79] One side is the inclinational will of God, and the other side is the intentional will of God. His intentional will is what he has determined will come to pass – such as Christ's ultimate and final victory over evil. His inclinational will is what he desires to accomplish but requires cooperation from man, such as Peter walking on water all the way to Jesus, rather than sinking halfway. DeArteaga insists:

> The incident where Peter walks on water is "especially instructive, because it is fatal to the sovereignty-only theory of Christian materialism. Although God's sovereignty and power (through Jesus) were the basis of Peter's water-walk, it was Peter's mind and spirit acting in faith, then fear, which determined the outcome."[80]

---

[78] McConnell, 152.

[79] King, 148.

[80] DeArteaga, 155.

As Andrew Murray wrote, "There is often great confusion as to the will of God. People think that what God wills must inevitably take place. This is by no means the case... Of God's will revealed in his promises, so much will be fulfilled as our faith accepts."[81]

So, to answer McConnell, a personal, loving God *does* determine what comes into a believer's life, just not in the rigid way that some seem to think. Since he predetermines what grace he makes available to us (which I will address in detail later), he also determines categorically what does not come into our lives. God also works very personally in each person, stirring desires to reach out for specific blessings. As Paul writes, "...for it is God who works in you, both to will and to work for his good pleasure" (Philippians 2:13). So, where some view sovereignty as God deciding in each moment what each should have, the Word of Faith sees that God has largely pre-decided to supply and is working in each one to draw their attention to himself and his blessings, at which point we reach out and receive them. As Hart explains, "As we take our ultimate joy and delight in God, he

---

[81] King, 196.

conforms our inmost desires to his holy will and our God-given dreams are realized."[82]

The main difference in the specific application of faith is whether faith is passive or active. A total sovereignty view tends to make faith primarily passive, because God is going to do what God is going to do. In contrast, a cooperative, or limited, sovereignty view recognizes that God wills good things for us, but we must join him on the adventure of faith if we are going to experience all he has in store. That said, in this more limited sovereignty view, there remains a definite place for acquiescing to the will of God in submitted consecration. As Hart notes, "Authentic faith is both dependence or reliance and obedience."[83]

Because the motif of the inheritance bestowed and the "past tense" play such a pivotal role in the Word of Faith movement's understanding of Scripture, these views lead to several of the other key doctrinal distinctives: 1. The focus on reading, studying, and hearing teaching of God's word to identify

---

[82] Larry D. Hart, *Truth Aflame* (Grand Rapids: Thomas Nelson, 1999), 412.

[83] Ibid.

what has been given. 2. The focus on discovering one's identity –
or "who you are in Christ" – to see oneself as God does, so the
hearer will believe they are worthy and able to receive the
inheritance. 3. The focus on the role and operation of faith, as the
spiritual hand that takes possession of the promises, including the
importance of acting and speaking in faith.

Hearing the Word

First, the Word of Faith movement is largely a teaching
movement because of Paul's words in Romans 10:17, "faith comes
from hearing, and hearing through the word of Christ." The
movement recognizes that proclamation of the truth is critical in
helping people to understand, believe, respond to, and experience
that truth. There is also an emphasis on teaching and hearing
continually, as Hagin notes: "That's the reason I keep teaching
certain truths over and over again. Folks don't get it just because
you say it once."[84,85]

---

[84] Hagin, *Bible Faith...*, Location 972.

[85] As a personal side note: During my journey of pursuing my
M.Div., I have also been leading a local church Bible school. That experience
has been eye-opening to me regarding the importance of verbal proclamation
of the Gospel. As an educated Westerner, I have often understood the words
"faith comes from hearing" in Romans 10:17 to include Bible reading.
However, seeing how many of our adult bible school students struggle with

Another text often quoted in the Word of Faith movement regarding teaching is Hosea 4:6a, "My people are destroyed for lack of knowledge…" The idea is that people often suffer in ways that are not according to the will of God because they are ignorant of what belongs to them in Christ. (In context, Hosea is condemning the priests for rejecting knowledge, which ultimately led to the ignorance of the people. However, regardless of the path that led them there, the result is the same.) This perspective serves as motivation behind the wide variety of avenues that major ministries use to get their teaching out to the public. Since people need to hear, and will suffer needlessly if they don't, teachers need to reach them and teach them using whatever means available.

The specific pattern, so prevalent in the WOF movement today, of building large, multimedia ministries, owes its invention to F.F. Bosworth (1877-1958). Bosworth was one of the founding fathers of the Assemblies of God and author of *Christ the Healer*,

---

reading difficulties has reminded me that this passage is specifically referring to verbal proclamation. It has helped to reaffirm the value of preaching in my eyes, as verbal proclamation provides the most basic way for the most people to hear, understand, be saved, and grow in their walk with Christ.

a popular book featured in Hagin's RBTC curriculum.[86] Perriman notes that it was Bosworth, whose use of radio, large campaigns, and extensive administrative staff "established a format for Pentecostal evangelistic organizations that was replicated to great effect by a multitude of successors."[87] This development had a profound impact on the movement's visibility and spread, increasing the audience of certain personalities who came to be identified as leaders.[88] As Harrison emphasizes, "Television's role…cannot be overstated."[89]

Because of this heavy emphasis on educating people in Scripture, leaders in the Word of Faith movement place a major emphasis on people bringing their Bibles to church. When I was growing up in 1980s, most of the audience would bring their Bible with them to church and conferences, often equipped with highlighters, pens, and notepads as well. As technology has

---

[86] The Azusa Street Revival, "F.F. Bosworth," accessed August 5, 2024, https://www.azusastreet.org/Participant_Bosworth_F_F.htm.

[87] Perriman, 63.

[88] Horvath, 9.

[89] Harrison, 161.

progressed, many churches have begun to display verses on their screens, though some hold back from this practice in a strategic effort to encourage their people to use their Bibles.

The rise of smartphone use and Bible apps has also led to concern among some WOF pastors and teachers. In several contexts where I have served, leaders have commented from the pulpit about how they tried using digital Bibles but have returned to the paper version, finding they can better concentrate on hearing from God when they are not focused on wrangling with technology.

Who You are in Christ

The second unique aspect of the Word of Faith teaching is its emphasis on discovering one's identity in Christ. As Harrison notes, "knowing 'who you are in Christ' is, according to those within the Word of Faith Movement, the key to living the higher Christian life."[90] Harrison adds, "Receiving this revelation of

---

[90] Harrison, 8.

one's rights and privileges as a new creation in Christ is the first step to success and abundant life in this world."[91]

And, indeed, this is recognized within the movement as the first thing a new Christian should learn. It is common in Word of Faith churches for new converts to be gifted Bibles, along with booklets that contain information regarding their new status as a child of God. In my dad's church, new believers currently receive a copy of *This New Life* by Billy Joe Daugherty, founder of Victory Church (formerly Victory Christian Center) in Tulsa, OK. Many churches in our movement offer booklets by Kenneth E. Hagin, including *The New Birth* and *In Him*. For example, when one responds to the altar call for salvation at a Kenneth Hagin Ministries conference, or at Rhema Bible Church, founded and led by Kenneth W. Hagin, Jr., they receive these booklets.[92]

Whether one receives *This New Life* or *The New Birth* and *In Him*, the central thrust of the content is based on 2 Corinthians

---

[91] Ibid., 9.

[92] Personal experience in the author's family. Present practice confirmed by the author with an employee of Kenneth Hagin Ministries on July 31, 2024.

5:17, "Therefore, if anyone is in Christ, he is a new creation. The old has passed away; behold, the new has come." The booklets serve to help the new convert begin to see themselves as the Bible describes them – not as they were before Christ, but as they now are "in him." The content emphasizes a clean break and a drastic change happening at conversion, rooted in having been born of God as his own child. As a child of God, the new convert has become an heir to God's blessings. As Hagin writes, "Being born again – becoming the child of God – is of foremost importance. It is the key that unlocks all the promises of God to you. For when you become a child of God – then God's promises become yours."[93]

Rooted in Jesus' teaching about being "born again" in John 3:1-15, Word of Faith teaching focuses on receiving a new nature. In *The New Birth*, Hagin illustrates it using the difference between a racehorse and a mule.[94] The point being that a mule can never perform like a racehorse, even when given a similar environment

---

[93] Kenneth E. Hagin, *The New Birth* (Tulsa: Kenneth Hagin Ministries, 1975), 24.

[94] Ibid., 12.

and training, because it is just not in him. To run like a racehorse, the mule would have to be reborn as one. Similarly, a sinner cannot achieve holiness. He or she must be reborn with a holy nature.

Olson notes that "Augustine wrote several treatises on original sin and inherited, total depravity. He argued that before the fall the human condition was *posse non peccare* (possible not to sin) but that after the fall our universal human condition is *non posse non peccare* (not possible not to sin)."[95] Carrying Augustine's progression through conversion then would necessitate a renewal that restores the individual to the "possible not to sin" condition. Seeming to confirm this, Irenaeus held that all who experience salvation in Christ are not only forgiven but renewed.[96] Olson underscores this idea, writing that the atoning work is not only an objective event, "but also a transforming event."[97]

---

[95] Roger E. Olson, *The Mosaic of Christian Belief* (Downers Grove: InterVarsity Press, 2016), 211.

[96] Ibid., 276.

[97] Ibid., 275.

The Word of Faith movement understands that Jesus was able to live sinless because he had a unique conception and birth. That explains why he has now made a new birth available to us. When we are born of the Spirit, we have renewed potential to live holy, like our Father is holy (Ephesians 5:1+, 1 Peter 1:15).

This is an area of doctrine related to the nature of humanity where Word of Faith teaching begins to diverge from some other evangelicals, even those who hold a strong faith emphasis. As King notes, classic faith leaders tended to teach that righteousness is *imputed*, whereas contemporary faith leaders, in line with Kenyon, tend to teach that righteousness is *imparted*.[98] This difference means that Word of Faith teaching describes a nature change – the spirit of man recreated, renewed in complete innocence with Christ's righteousness – whereas others see righteousness as something with which the believer is merely clothed, leaving his or her core nature untouched.

Oden describes this process, writing: "Regeneration is the work of the Spirit by which new life in Christ is *imparted* to one

---

[98] King, 88.

dead in sin" (emphasis added).[99] Completing the circle, Hubbard points out that "'Spirit' and 'life' are virtual synonyms in Paul.[100] Therefore, one can say that, at conversion, God imparts a new spirit, which results in a new life, a renewed inner nature.

The Word of Faith logic follows the progression of Paul's discussion in 2 Corinthians 5. In verse 12, Paul makes a distinction between the outward appearance and the heart. In verse 16, he makes a similar distinction, referring to how they previously judged Christ "according to the flesh" but "we regard him thus no longer." In both cases, the outer precedes the inner, the lower to the higher. This order mirrors that of Jesus' statement to Nicodemus regarding conversion in John 3:6, "That which is born of the flesh is flesh, and that which is born of the Spirit is spirit." The fleshly or material precedes the inner or spiritual.

Paul continues in verse 17: "Therefore, if anyone is in Christ, he is a new creation. The old has passed away; behold, the

---

[99] Thomas C. Oden, *Classic Christianity* (New York: HarperCollins, 1992), 612.

[100] Moyer V. Hubbard, *New Creation in Paul's Letters and Thought* (Cambridge: Cambridge University Press, 2002), 90.

new has come." Paul makes the new creation intensely personal, saying that the convert "*is* a new creation" (emphasis added), not that they are surrounded by new possibilities or given new potential (though these things may also follow as benefits of the renewal).

To confirm what aspect of the person is recreated, we can apply Jesus' statement of order in John 3:6. We came into the world born of the flesh, our first birth. So, when we have been reborn, our second – or subsequent – birth, we have been born of the Spirit. And since Christ explained that "that which is born of the Spirit is spirit," we know that the convert has been spiritually reborn.

As we come to verse 21, Paul reveals that Christ became sin so that "we might become the righteousness of God." Since this is described in the context of Paul's discussion of what we have *become* (new creatures, ambassadors for Christ, righteousness of God), the Word of Faith movement understands this as an impartation of a righteous nature.

Understanding that one has been made new on the inside, on the spiritual level, is critical to the Word of Faith concept of discipleship, which primarily means learning to identify with, and live out of, this new nature. Rather than focusing on binding, washing, or masking the old nature, the WOF focuses on feeding, strengthening, and activating the new nature. For example, Hagin writes, "God's nature is love. As His child you have the love nature in you. Yet that nature has to be fed in order for it to grow. Unless you feed where this is found [scriptures about love], it will not grow and develop in your life."[101]

All this falls under the broad heading of learning "who you are in Christ." As previously mentioned, many Word of Faith churches use Hagin's booklet *In Him*. This little booklet presents dozens of scriptures in the New Testament that talk about who believers are or what they have, "in Christ," "in him," "by him," "through him," etc. The core idea is that believers in Christ have put away their old life and have received a new life, which is Christ living in them:

> For through the law I died to the law, so that I might live to God. I have been crucified with Christ. It is no longer I who live, but Christ who lives in me. And the life I now

---

[101] Kenneth E. Hagin, *Growing up Spiritually* (Tulsa: Kenneth Hagin Ministries, 1976), 143.

live in the flesh I live by faith in the Son of God, who loved me and gave himself for me. (Galatians 2:19-20)

Here we see that our identity as Christians is no longer tied primarily to who we *were* before conversion, as that person was crucified with Christ (made effective in the present through one's faith). Now a believer's identity is tied to Christ – his righteousness, his position of favor with the Father, and his exalted place of authority over all the powers of darkness.

Ephesians 1 proves central in this discussion as well, especially Paul's prayer in verses 16-23. Key to the concept of identity in Christ is the statement that Christ has been seated "at his right hand in the heavenly places, far above all rule and authority and power and dominion" (vv. 20-21). This is connected to the individual believer by the fact that the Father "gave him as head over all things to the church, which is his body, the fullness of him who fills all in all" (vv. 22-23). Christ being the head recognizes his unique authority over the church. However, the church as his fullness reflects how the head and the body share one nature, as parts of one whole. As our old nature died with him (Romans 6:8-11), we were filled with Christ as we were raised with him.

This is to say that there is both unity and distinction: Though the believer is joined to Christ spiritually (1 Corinthians 6:17), there is a recognition that the believer is not on the same level as the second person of the Godhead. As Hagin writes:

> …the Church is called Christ! The Church has not yet realized that we are Christ. No, we're not divine as He is, but we are joint heirs with Him – we are His body sent forth to work in the earth on His behalf….The believer is called Christ! We are identified with Him! The church is called *believers*. The church is called *righteousness*. The church is called *light*. The church is called *Christ*! That's who we are!... Christ is the head; we are the body. We are one with Christ. We are not gods, but we've been given the right to use Jesus' Name, and to act on His behalf.[102]

So, just as Jesus said, "I am the light of the world" (John 8:12) and told his disciples, "You are the light of the world" (Matthew 5:14), the Word of Faith concept of identification sees that Christ is living in the believer and filling the believer with his nature. Without Christ's light, we cannot be light. Without Christ's righteousness, we cannot be righteous. However, because we are his Body, we have both – plus much more.

---

[102] Kenneth E. Hagin, *The Name of Jesus* (Tulsa: Kenneth Hagin Ministries, 1979), 105-6.

Spirit, Soul, and Body

This then leads us to another aspect of identity, of "who you are in Christ," that is a key doctrine of the Word of Faith movement. That is the position that we are made in the image and likeness of God; therefore, we are spiritual beings.

This idea is rooted in Genesis 1:26-27:

> 26 Then God said, "Let us make man in our image, after our likeness. And let them have dominion over the fish of the sea and over the birds of the heavens and over the livestock and over all the earth and over every creeping thing that creeps on the earth."
> 27 So God created man in his own image,
>   in the image of God he created him;
>   male and female he created them.

Scripture teaches that God created humans in his "image" and "likeness." However, theologians often struggle to define what that exactly means. Olson notes that this "has been the subject of much disagreement and debate, and the source of diversity within the Christian consensus."[103]

This diversity arouses debate here as well: Perriman notes that the Word of Faith movement understands Adam's creation of

---

[103] Olson, 208.

the image of God to mean that there is a much stronger resemblance between the Creator and the creature than most evangelicals would espouse.[104] Bowman, expounding on this idea, writes, "...the Word-Faith teachers insist that human beings are much more like God than Christians have usually believed. Our creation in God's image is interpreted to mean that we exist in God's 'class,' as the same kind of being as God, though on a smaller scale..."[105]

Confirming this, Hagin writes: "We know that man is a spirit because he is in the same class as God. Man is made in the image and the likeness of God (Gen. 1:26)....It is not your physical man that is like God, for the Bible says that God is not a man (Num. 23:19)."[106] In another place, Hagin says, "Man is a spirit being. He is made in the likeness of God. Jesus said that God is a Spirit (John 4:24). So man must of necessity be a spirit."[107]

---

[104] Perriman, 19-20.

[105] Bowman, 32.

[106] Hagin, *Bible Faith...*, Location 1868.

[107] Kenneth E. Hagin, *How You Can Be Led by the Spirit of God* (Tulsa: Kenneth Hagin Ministries, 1978), 3.

Another view that appears often in theology is the "metaphysical" view. In this view, humans are like God because we are creatures capable of reason and righteousness – we can discern and choose between right and wrong.[108] Bowman echoes that view, though he calls it "moral likeness." He explains that human beings were created as physical *representations* of God in the world, much like a Roman coin would bear Caesar's image, while pointing out that the coin would not carry Caesar's nature.[109] By this, Bowman does not mean that our physical bodies look like God in some way; rather, that we carry out God's purposes in this physical world. Since we carry out God's purposes, Bowman also sees a "functional" likeness in how humans were created to exercise dominion on the earth, mirroring God's own dominion.

Though Bowman argues against the Word of Faith view that humans were created as spirits, he does note that we were uniquely "meant to live forever, to know God personally."[110] This

---

[108] Daniel J. Treier, *Introducing Evangelical Theology* (Grand Rapids: Baker Academic, 2019), 148.

[109] Bowman, 136.

[110] Ibid.

unique eternal nature and relational compatibility with God, contrasted against all other life on earth, would seem to indicate that Bowman has painted the silhouette of the spiritual nature of man without noticing that he did. Furthermore, where Bowman stops short of recognizing a likeness of nature, Olson seems to agree with Hagin on that premise. Though he makes a point of emphasizing a strong distinction between the essence of God and humans, Olson does discuss the "spirit of a person."[111]

For clarity's sake, I should also mention that Word of Faith teachers don't exclude or oppose the metaphysical and functional views mentioned above. In agreement with other Christian groups, we also see humans as reasoning, moral, and entrusted with dominion. However, Word of Faith teaching generally emphasizes the spiritual dimension and includes the moral and functional aspects as flowing from, or complementary to, the spiritual.

Where one finds even more contention between those inside and outside of the Word of Faith movement surrounds the

---

[111] Olson, 205.

discussion of the makeup of a human being and how different aspects, or parts, of human nature should be identified or prioritized. Where many Christians see humans as a single unit (monistic view), and others see humans as the synergy or union of soul and body (dualistic view), Word of Faith teachers present the human being as spirit, soul, and body (trichotomous view).

Often, one of the first verses presented by Word of Faith teachers when discussing this subject is 1 Thessalonians 5:23, "Now may the God of peace himself sanctify you completely, and may your whole spirit and soul and body be kept blameless at the coming of our Lord Jesus Christ." In the second chapter of Hagin's *How You Can Be Led By The Spirit of God*, this verse follows directly after his use of Genesis 1:26-27 and John 4:24 as he presents his view of human nature. Commenting on it, he states what is perhaps the most unique assertion of this teaching in Word of Faith circles, when compared with others who are open to trichotomy: "Man is a spirit, and he has a soul, and he lives in a physical body."[112]

---

[112] Hagin, *How You…*, 3.

This statement deserves special attention because Hagin does not say that humans have a spirit, soul, and body. He states that the human essentially *is* a spirit. As Bowman notes, "...the statement, so common in Kenyon and the Word-Faith teachers, [is] that the 'real man' is the inner one, the spirit."[113]

So, not only do Word of Faith teachers generally hold to a trichotomous view of human nature, but they also hold to a view where the spirit of man is prioritized as the most essential, as the core nature or identity of a human being. Discussing what it means to believe with the heart (Romans 10:10), Hagin explains:

> The word "heart" is used to convey a thought. Notice how we use the word "heart" today. We talk about the heart of a tree. What do we mean? We mean the center, the very core. We talk about the heart of a subject. What do we mean? We mean the most important part of that subject— the very center of it—the main part of it around which the rest revolves.
>
> And when God speaks of the human heart, He is speaking about the main part of man, the very center of man's being, which is his spirit.[114]

---

[113] Bowman, 73.

[114] Hagin, *Bible Faith...*, Location 1854.

Hagin argues further for the priority of the spirit, noting that the spirit is listed first (in 1 Thess. 5:23), but most people would probably turn the order around because "Natural things mean more to them than spiritual things."[115]

Critics often point out that the list of parts of a human being in 1 Thessalonians 5 is likely a word salad, rather than a definitive list. It is usually compared with Mark 12:30, "And you shall love the Lord your God with all your heart and with all your soul and with all your mind and with all your strength."

The word salad argument asserts that such lists are not meant to be definitive. Rather, they use various, but related descriptive words simply for the point of emphasis. A more modern-day example of a word salad would be, "I will love you every second, of every minute, of every hour, of every day…," which would also include every month, year, decade, etc., without indicating that time only has four units of measurement.

Interestingly, in Mark 12, Jesus is quoting Deuteronomy 6, which includes only heart, soul, and might – which would better

---

[115] Hagin, *How You…*, 9.

align with 1 Thessalonians 5. However, Jesus adds "mind" to the list, seemingly for more emphasis.

And while I can readily concede that the word salad view may have merit, it cannot account for other places in Scripture where trichotomy seems clear or necessary. First, there are many deeper questions regarding the application of redemptive renewal that would seem to point to a trichotomous view. Secondly, how Paul teaches the application of spiritual gifts makes a further critical distinction.

We have already discussed (at least partially) what it means to be born again. When one is born of the Spirit, there is an impartation of a new life, a complete transformation at the spiritual level that results in a new creation/creature (2 Corinthians 5:17). Also, note 1 Peter 1:23, "since you have been born again, not of perishable seed but of imperishable, through the living and abiding word of God." So, Paul, Peter, and Jesus (through John) all reference a new birth, a one-time event, that completely transforms a person on the inside. Peter makes it clear that this event happened at a point in the past for his audience of the "elect" (1 Peter 1:1). So, we can say that, for a believer, the primary redemptive renewal of the spirit happened at a past point in this life – at conversion.

There is also a clear redemptive renewal that will occur in the future. Paul paints a clear picture for his readers in 1 Corinthians 15:50-53.

> 50 I tell you this, brothers: flesh and blood cannot inherit the kingdom of God, nor does the perishable inherit the imperishable. 51 Behold! I tell you a mystery. We shall not all sleep, but we shall all be changed, 52 in a moment, in the twinkling of an eye, at the last trumpet. For the trumpet will sound, and the dead will be raised imperishable, and we shall be changed. 53 For this perishable body must put on the imperishable, and this mortal body must put on immortality.

Paul underscores that this takes place in the future, writing: "And not only the creation, but we ourselves, who have the firstfruits of the Spirit, groan inwardly as we wait eagerly for adoption as sons, the redemption of our bodies" (Romans 8:23).

Note that Paul specifically calls the coming transformation the "redemption of our bodies." We have already seen how redemption impacts our inner person, which is in the past tense for anyone who has placed their faith in Christ. Now we see that redemption will be fully realized in our outer person on the day of Christ's return. So, we see two different aspects of human nature that are impacted by redemption, at two different times, which are both sudden and transformative.

At first glance, this would seem to fit with a dichotomous view. However, Scripture also speaks of a third renewal, which fits with the tense that we have not yet discussed – the present. We see this discussed in Romans 12:

> I appeal to you therefore, brothers, by the mercies of God, to present your bodies as a living sacrifice, holy and acceptable to God, which is your spiritual worship. Do not be conformed to this world, but be transformed by the renewal of your mind, that by testing you may discern what is the will of God, what is good and acceptable and perfect. (Romans 12:1-2)

Here, Paul discusses that we are to present our *bodies* as sacrifices to God, which is our *spiritual* worship, covering the two parts we have already mentioned. However, he also talks about another aspect of redemptive renewal that is unique, in that it is not sudden, but ongoing: That is the "renewal of your mind" (v.2).

Just as one immediately notices that their body was not changed by coming to faith in Christ, one also notices that their memories are still intact. A new Christian still knows how to read (if they did before), knows their name, etc. Whereas, on the spiritual level, "all things are made new," on the mental level, all things remain the same. Because they were unchanged by the new birth, one's thoughts and assumptions must be proactively renewed *after* conversion to align with the truth. Paul explains that this makes the believer able to "discern the will of God" (v.2). He calls this process the "renewal of your mind." The goal is to think godly, so one can talk godly, and walk godly – just like Jesus did.[116]

Hagin underscores the importance of this process:

We renew our minds by studying the word of God. The Bible teaches us to have "the mind of Christ" (1 Cor. 2:16). The only way we can have the mind of Christ is to study His Word, believe it in our heart, and act upon it.

The word of God also teaches us to think on whatever is true, honest, just, pure, lovely, a good report, or whatever has virtue or praise (Phil. 4:8). So the Word of God does have much to say about the mind![117]

---

[116] Harrison, 214.

[117] Kenneth E. Hagin, *Right and Wrong Thinking* (Tulsa: Kenneth Hagin Ministries, 1966), 4.

Hagin also emphasizes that our mind is critical to our walk of faith. He explains that "our believing is the result of our right or wrong thinking."[118]

So, where the spirit was renewed (past tense), and the body will eventually be renewed (future tense), it is the responsibility of the believer to take up the lifelong process of renewing the mind (present tense). This would seem to support the trichotomous view.

The other application that makes a mind/spirit distinction is Paul's instruction about tongues in 1 Cor 14:

> 13 Therefore, one who speaks in a tongue should pray that he may interpret. 14 For if I pray in a tongue, my spirit prays but my mind is unfruitful. 15 What am I to do? I will pray with my spirit, but I will pray with my mind also; I will sing praise with my spirit, but I will sing with my mind also.

Important here is the way that Paul distinguishes between the spirit and the mind. In this context, the spirit and mind are operating *independently*. In verse 14, the spirit prays or sings, while the mind

---

[118] Ibid., 17.

remains unfruitful. In verse 15, the spirit prays and sings alone, and then is joined by the mind when Paul chooses.

Furthermore, Paul states in v.14 that, when he prays in tongues, his "spirit prays." Acts 2:4 tells us that those on the Day of Pentecost were able "to speak in other tongues as the Spirit gave them utterance." So, Paul and Luke understand that, when praying/speaking in tongues, a person is speaking from their spirit by the Holy Spirit. This Spirit-to-spirit connection would seem to confirm Hagin's position that being created in the image of God includes being made as a spiritual being.

So, because redemption seems to be applied to three different parts of a human being at three different times and in three different ways, and because Paul distinguishes between spirit and mind, it seems most appropriate, and most practical, to view a human being through the lens of trichotomy, as Hagin describes in terms of spirit, soul, and body.

In this discussion, I have pointed out two arguments related to the spirit and the "mind," not the "soul" – the term Hagin includes in his initial description. However, Hagin includes the mind as *part* of the soul. He explains, "the soul is made up of the mind, will, and emotions."[119] So, while presenting enough evidence regarding the mind to establish the distinction, I will not address the emotions or will for the sake of brevity.

However, though I, and Word of Faith teachers in general, see the most truth and value in the tripartite definition, I have come to appreciate that the monistic and dualistic approaches also have merit in appropriate settings. It can prove very helpful to consider this discussion from all three viewpoints.

Perriman argues that "Biblical anthropology remains fundamentally monistic and holistic."[120] I find it interesting that he uses the word "fundamentally," seeming to recognize some distinction while emphasizing integration. This reflects the reality that we experience life as a human being, not as a disembodied spirit or separated intellect. This also mirrors what Hagin would repeatedly emphasize when discussing the parts of our nature live, insisting that "you can separate them for the sake of study," but that we live our lives with all of our parts working together.

---

[119] Hagin, *Bible Faith…*, Location 2024.

[120] Perriman, 127.

In a similar vein, McConnell argues, the body "is the living form of that self, the necessary expression of our individual existence."[121] While Word of Faith teaching sees the body as subject to the spirit and mind, we also recognize that God created humans with a body, and the body was included in the Creation that God judged as "very good" (Gen. 1:31). Therefore, the body must be regarded as a wonderful and necessary part of our being. We also read in 1 Cor. 15 that in the age to come we will continue to have a body, though not this mortal one. Therefore, though our present body is contaminated with the nature of sin, it remains a valuable part of our being, an instrument with which we express our worship to God and execute His will on the earth. For this reason, we must nourish and cherish it, as Paul describes in Ephesians 5:29.

While there is a way in which we can and should view humans as an integrated whole, Scripture also presents a duality of the inner and outer, a distinction between our visible and

---

[121] McConnell,144.

invisible parts. Possibly the most pointed example is Jesus' words in Matthew 26:14, where he tells his disciples, "Watch and pray that you may not enter into temptation. The spirit indeed is willing, but the flesh is weak." He also confronts the Pharisees with this clarification: "Do you not see that whatever goes into the mouth passes into the stomach and is expelled? But what comes out of the mouth proceeds from the heart, and this defiles a person" (Matthew 15:17-18). Furthermore, to clarify that this idea is not confined to Matthew: Paul describes an experience of a man (presumably himself) who "was caught up to the third heaven— whether in the body or out of the body I do not know, God knows" (2 Corinthians 12:2). He also writes in 2 Corinthians 4:16, "So we do not lose heart. Though our outer self is wasting away, our inner self is being renewed day by day."

Therefore, there are times when it makes sense to speak of the human being as a single unit and times when it makes sense to speak of the visible and invisible parts. I have already presented the standard Word of Faith view of the tripartite nature of man, which demonstrates that this view is biblically justified and, at times, practically necessary.

Since these views each have their place, it seems to be that we should give other saints grace when they choose to prefer a certain paradigm. For example, like Perriman's attitude regarding monism, Bowman is diplomatic regarding his dualistic view: "In my opinion, dualism is basically correct, but there are things to be learned from trichotomy. And there is not enough to go on to be dogmatic about the matter or to regard either dualism or trichotomism as aberrant or heretical."[122]

All that said, the Word of Faith movement emphasizes the trichotomy approach because it was the way that Hagin presented it. It also seems to provide the best foundation to clearly discuss the elements of human nature most distinctly, while faithfully relaying Scripture's prioritization of the spiritual:

> "Do not lay up for yourselves treasures on earth, where moth and rust destroy and where thieves break in and steal, but lay up for yourselves treasures in heaven, where neither moth nor rust destroys and where thieves do not break in and steal. 21 For where your treasure is, there your heart will be also. (Matthew 6:19-20)

---

[122] Bowman, 102.

for while bodily training is of some value, godliness is of value in every way, as it holds promise for the present life and also for the life to come. (1 Timothy 4:8)

For we do not wrestle against flesh and blood, but against the rulers, against the authorities, against the cosmic powers over this present darkness, against the spiritual forces of evil in the heavenly places. (Ephesians 6:12)

Scripture's prioritization of the spiritual undergirds Hagin's reading of 1 Corinthians 9:27, "But I discipline my body and keep it under control, lest after preaching to others I myself should be disqualified." Hagin understands this text to say that Paul does not identify with his body as being his person, since Paul uses the possessive pronoun, calling it "my body." Therefore, since the body is not the center of personhood, and the spirit is prioritized, Hagin sees the spirit as the center of personal identity. Accordingly, Hagin and the Word of Faith movement in general teach: "Man is a spirit. He has a soul. He lives in a body."[123]

Now, some argue that Paul also uses the possessive pronoun when talking about his spirit and soul. We already read 1 Corinthians 14:15, "What am I to do? I will pray with my spirit,

---

[123] Hagin, *How You...*, 3.

but I will pray with my mind also; I will sing praise with my spirit, but I will sing with my mind also." Therefore, for Hagin to insist, based solely on 1 Cor. 9:27, that the spirit should be one's primary identity would seem short-sighted, especially considering a holistic view, where a human is a human, which includes all the parts.

However, Hagin's approach seems to have functional, instructional merit while mirroring Paul's approach in other passages. For example, looking again to 2 Corinthians 5, we read, "From now on, therefore, we regard no one according to the flesh. Even though we once regarded Christ according to the flesh, we regard him thus no longer" (v.16). In other words, the lens through which some perceived and identified Christ was through the natural lens of a Jewish son of a carpenter, born of questionable legitimacy, without the customary theological training, etc. Paul, however, is pointing out that identifying Christ through those means causes problems and does not accurately represent his actual person. It also obscures his position in relation to God, humanity, and the rest of the spiritual world. In other words, though they once judged Christ in the natural, the better way to know, understand, or identify Christ is according to spiritual realities.

And these realities are revealed about him in Scripture - through prophecy, through the incarnation, through his words, through the words of the Father, and through what was revealed and written through the apostles. For example, with our eyes, we do not see Christ as highly exalted and seated at the right hand of the Father. Those kinds of realities, though clearly true about Christ, cannot be ascertained using physical means or human reasoning. They can only be "revealed from faith for faith," as Paul describes in Romans 1:16-17.

> For I am not ashamed of the gospel, for it is the power of God for salvation to everyone who believes, to the Jew first and also to the Greek. For in it the righteousness of God is revealed from faith for faith, as it is written, "The righteous shall live by faith."

Therefore, if Christ is best known by what the Gospel says about him, because physical senses and mental reasoning cannot discern it, it would follow that a Christian is also best known by what they read about themselves in Scripture, since our new selves cannot be known by other means.

This reality would also seem to make the spiritual part of us, as the first part that redemption transforms, the primary one in the eyes of God. For these reasons, then, it seems biblically justified for Hagin to place the seat of identity in the spiritual aspect of our makeup and state that "Man is a spirit. He has a soul. He lives in a body."

This view also helps the individual believer to see him- or herself based on what Christ has accomplished in them by his Spirit at the new birth. Since that transformation, and the possibilities it opens, can only be known through the revelation contained in Scripture, seeing oneself in Scripture becomes essential to knowing oneself and to growing spiritually. In 2 Cor. 3:18, Paul explains that as we are "beholding the glory of the Lord, are being transformed into the same image from one degree of glory to another." To see Christ's holiness, love, etc., is to see one's new nature and grow in the faith necessary to live this out in daily life.

So, identifying oneself as spiritual impacts the overall Word of Faith model of spiritual growth for all three parts of human nature: Feeding the spirit with the Word of God results in spiritual strength and faith to live daily life in Christ. This approach also helps the believer to understand their responsibility to do something with their mind (to renew it) and with their body (to discipline it).

These sum up many of the key concepts related to what the Word of Faith teaches about "who you are in Christ." This new view of oneself is critical for a believer, so they will not fall under the condemnation of the enemy and talk themselves out of the blessings that God has provided for them, which they now can and should possess by faith.

The Operation of Faith

Introducing Faith

As mentioned previously, Hagin recounted how he had received his healing through a revelation of faith, and how God called him to "teach my people faith." Because of these experiences, his ministry focused on teaching people how to receive from God by using their faith, and that teaching serves as the foundation for the Word of Faith movement we see today.

That said, it is also clear that the Word of Faith movement does not somehow "own" the subject of faith. Faith plays a central role in Scripture and historically orthodox Christian doctrine in general. For example, Oden writes, quoting Chrysostom (4th century): "Faith is the primary condition for the reception of every subsequent stage of God's saving activity."[124] He also cites Bede (turn of the 8th century), explaining, "The life of faith that is commanded in the New Testament is not simply a single fleeting act, but rather an entire way of life, a way of walking by trusting in God continually."[125]

Furthermore, while popular television ministries tend to focus on a narrower subject area, it should be noted that Word of Faith churches teach much more than just faith. Kenneth W. Hagin, Jr., Pastor of Rhema Bible Church and current President of Kenneth Hagin Ministries, has often appealed for even greater balance among those who teach faith, reminding his audience that "the faith message is not the only message in the word of God."[126] However, while it doesn't own faith or only teach faith, the Word

---

[124] Oden, 598.

[125] Oden, 601.

[126] Perriman, 216.

of Faith movement does place a unique emphasis on the centrality of its role in the Christian life, which we will discuss in this section.

As previously mentioned, the core Scriptures that serve as the focus of the Word of Faith teaching are Mark 11:22-24. Having already quoted Hagin's preferred KJV, here is the ESV text:

> 22 And Jesus answered them, "Have faith in God. 23 Truly, I say to you, whoever says to this mountain, 'Be taken up and thrown into the sea,' and does not doubt in his heart, but believes that what he says will come to pass, it will be done for him. 24 Therefore I tell you, whatever you ask in prayer, believe that you have received it, and it will be yours.

Hagin was healed after 16 months bedridden as he took these words seriously and quite literally.[127] His teaching and that of the modern Word of Faith movement continue to take this stance regarding the literal possibility of receiving answers to prayer and seeing the miraculous occur in response to taking God at his word.

---

[127] Hagin, *Bible Faith...*, Location 697.

As Hagin has noted, this text in Mark 11 describes the "unalterable law of faith."[128]

While some take issue with Hagin's use of the word "law" here and the Word of Faith's use of the concept of spiritual laws in general, it should be noted that this is not a new idea in Christian theology. DeArteaga explains:

> The understanding of the reliability of God's promises is an element of evangelical theology of long standing. We agree with it completely. But notice, if God's promises are reliable because of His character, they will always be executed when humans meet their conditions. If this is the case, then there is only a semantic difference between God's promises and spiritual laws. In fact, one might be defined in terms of the other: The key element is that God's character is so righteous, and His power so awesome, that *His promises to behave as laws.*

King also notes the cause-and-effect relationship between God speaking and our responding to his word that forms the basis of what today is often taught as "spiritual laws" goes back to the teaching of Johannes Cocceius in the 17th century.[129]

---

[128] Kenneth E. Hagin, *Foundations for Faith* (Tulsa: Kenneth Hagin Ministries, 1998), 59.

[129] King, 34

Though some would find Jesus' words in Mark 11 intimidating and attempt to water down his intent, Perriman notes that when it comes to faith, "we cannot ignore the fact that the New Testament sets the bar very high."[130] In the context of Mark 11, Jesus had cursed the fig tree (v.14) and the disciples had just noticed that it withered as commanded (v.20). When Peter points this out to Jesus (v.21), Jesus' response is instructive: He does not point to his glory as God in the flesh. He could have said, "Of course it worked! I'm Divine. Don't try this at home!" Instead, Jesus takes the exact opposite approach – affirming the disciples' potential by instructing them to do similar works themselves.

Jesus begins with the imperative "Have faith in God" (v.22). Since the understood subject of Jesus' statement would be "you," he is clearly saying that the disciples – the average, messy human beings right in front of him – were capable of doing what he was describing here. As he proceeds to talk about moving mountains, receiving answers to prayer, and forgiving one's

---

[130] Perriman, 155.

93

neighbor (v.25), one understands that Jesus believes that his followers can (and should) do these things. This sense is supported by Jesus' statement in John 14:12, "Truly, truly, I say to you, whoever believes in me will also do the works that I do; and greater works than these will he do, because I am going to the Father."

What we have to consider with Jesus' acts and words in Mark 11 is the difference between a performance and a demonstration. We have all seen performances, either live or on TV, where someone has warned the viewers, "Do not try this at home!" With those words, they clarify that they are professionals, and they do not intend for anyone to attempt what they are about to do. They are putting on a performance for entertainment purposes only.

Contrast this with demonstrations you may see at school in art class, wood shop, or home economics courses. (Many schools have dropped these programs in recent years, but I think you get my point anyway.) The teacher will show the students how to do something, with the expressed intent that the student will soon follow their example and do it themselves. Whether that takes the form of using a potter's wheel to mold clay, using a power saw to cut lumber, or preheating the oven for a tray of muffins, what the teacher does is a demonstration for the students to emulate. Rather than warning the students not to try it, they are urging the students to take notes because they will soon be doing the same thing themselves.

In Jesus' case, we have to ask ourselves if he was putting on a performance or giving the disciples a demonstration. We can clearly see the distinction in his response. When Peter pointed out the withered fig tree, Jesus did not respond, "I am the greatest! Be amazed! But do not try this at home!" No, he launched into instructions about how to accomplish similar feats using their own faith. Jesus clearly meant this scenario as a demonstration.

Accordingly, the Word of Faith movement teaches people how to effectively use their faith as Jesus instructed in Mark 11. However, the Word of Faith movement recognizes the role of faith as much more pervasive than what is described in Mark 11. For example, faith's influential role is underscored by the fact that:

- Without faith it's impossible to please God. (Heb 11:5,6)
- We're saved (justified) by faith. (Rom 5:1, Eph 2:8)
- We walk by faith. (2 Cor. 5:7)

- We live by faith. (Rom. 1:17, Hab. 2:4)
- Faith … *works.* (Gal. 5:6)
- Faith is the victory that overcomes the world. (1 John 5:4)
- We have the spirit of faith (2 Cor. 4:13), the *same* spirit of faith...we believe and therefore speak.[131]

And there are many more examples throughout Scripture. However, the last one on this list deserves particular attention, because the name "Word of Faith" comes from the unique emphasis the movement places on the combination of believing and speaking. These two things are understood to work together to enable a person to experience all that God has prepared for them.

Hagin writes:

One day as I was reading [Mark 11:23] and meditating on it, the Holy Ghost brought to my attention that in this text Jesus mentions believing one time, and He mentions saying three times. Then the Lord said to me, "You will have to do three times as much preaching about the saying part as you do about the believing part. Folks are not missing it primarily in the believing part; they are missing it in the saying part."[132]

---

[131] Loren Hirschy, "BIG ROCKS" LBA FAITH FOUNDATIONS Course 9/2020, PDF.

[132] Hagin, *Bible Faith…*, Location 2957.

This is one reason why the Word of Faith movement places a strong emphasis on what people say, often referred to as their "confession."[133] Hagin further emphasizes its role, writing, "Confession is faith's way of expressing itself."[134] However, as this statement also illustrates, the speaking part must be an expression of faith – meaning that faith must exist *first*, so it can be expressed. So, before we dive into the Word of Faith teaching on words/confession, we must look at the teaching regarding the faith that it expresses.

Hagin has often structured his teaching on faith around answering key questions related to faith's nature and operation, including how faith comes, what faith is, what it means to believe with the heart, and how to turn your faith loose. Since this was his approach, and he is the architect behind the movement's teaching, we will follow it in our discussion as well.

---

[133] Ibid., Location 3007.

[134] Ibid., Location 3496.

How Faith Comes

Hagin bases his instruction regarding *how faith comes* on Romans 10:17, "So faith comes from hearing, and hearing through the word of Christ." As Paul emphasizes the necessity of hearing about Christ to believe on him and be saved, Hagin describes that faith for all of God's blessings comes the same way:

> In the gospel of Jesus Christ, there is provision for every need—salvation, deliverance, safety, preservation, healing, and soundness. Whatever need you have, the faith to receive your answer comes from hearing the Word of God. As you determine to feed upon the Word continually, you will see your faith grow to be able to receive the wonderful promises God has provided for His children.

Hagin points out that, since God requires us to have faith, then he must provide us a means to receive faith. Otherwise, he would be unjust.[135] However, since God has provided us a means to receive faith and commanded us to have it (Mark 11:22), the responsibility for faith now rests with us.[136]

Hagin continues this line of thought, explaining that, since God has provided a means for getting faith, he can fairly require

---

[135] Hagin, *Bible Faith...*, Location 26.

[136] Ibid.

it. For example, since James instructed elders to pray the prayer of faith for healing, elders must necessarily possess the faith to pray that prayer. If they are expected to possess it, God must have provided a means to attain it.[137]

Hagin also explains that, though he was eventually healed of his blood condition and paralysis, that did not happen until he came to God in faith as God's word both instructs and requires. He writes, "When I was trying to get healed, I cried and prayed, and said, 'Dear Lord, please heal me.' I begged Him to heal me, and prayed all night several nights, and nearly all night several other nights....but I wasn't getting any results."[138] It was only, as he explains, once he "learned what it means to have faith and to act on my faith" from Mark 11:24 that he received his healing and was out of his bed in a matter of minutes.[139]

Hagin taught that faith comes by hearing for everything that God wants us to receive, not just salvation/conversion. He

---

[137] Hagin, *Bible Faith...*, Location 118.

[138] Ibid., Location 804.

[139] Ibid., Location 937.

often explained this using Mark 5 – the account of the woman with the issue of blood.[140]

> 25 And there was a woman who had had a discharge of blood for twelve years, 26 and who had suffered much under many physicians, and had spent all that she had, and was no better but rather grew worse. 27 She had heard the reports about Jesus and came up behind him in the crowd and touched his garment. 28 For she said, "If I touch even his garments, I will be made well." 29 And immediately the flow of blood dried up, and she felt in her body that she was healed of her disease.... 34 And he said to her, "Daughter, your faith has made you well; go in peace, and be healed of your disease."

Commenting on this account, he points out that Jesus said her faith had healed her. He asks, "Where did this woman get faith to receive healing? She got faith when she "...had heard of Jesus..."[141]

Hagin and other teachers within the movement point out that hearing God's word is the scriptural way to receive faith. Though people often pray for more faith, or passively wait for God

---

[140] Hagin, *Bible Faith...*, in this book alone, Hagin references this story 19 different times.

[141] Ibid., Location 194.

to drop it on them, that's not what Scripture teaches. If we are going to receive faith biblically or strengthen the faith we have, we must turn to God's word, exercising due diligence to cooperate with the principle that he has revealed.

As we come to God's word, we must also remember that we are not just seeking to learn information *about* God. God's word is the message of *Christ*, of a vital relationship between the Savior and his Church. As DeArteaga asserts, "At the core of the Christian's life is the relationship of creature to Creator, of dependent child to loving Father, which is intensely personal, not mechanical."[142] A.B. Simpson wrote, "true faith is not believing in words merely, even divine words, but believing ON the Lord Jesus Christ."[143] Echoing this idea, Murray taught, "Faith in the promise is the fruit of faith in the promiser."[144] So when we're talking about Bible faith, it's about living faith in, with, and through Christ.

---

[142] DeArteaga, 158.

[143] King, 177.

[144] Ibid.

Hart notes a balance here, explaining that "true faith brings us into personal union with Christ. It is not merely a set of beliefs about Christ."[145] At the same time, however, "faith always has content."[146]

This is critical to mention because even in the early Church's struggle for doctrinal formation, they began to focus "on questions about the nature of the trinity, and the personhood of Christ, and of the Holy Spirit, rather than on daily living in the Spirit."[147] DeArteaga explains that this led to a situation where, during the first five centuries of the Church, "the unintended consequence was a shift in the understanding of faith away from faith-expectancy to faith-doctrine."[148]

And this shift has continued to exercise influence throughout Church history. It was further exacerbated by the fact that Calvin wanted to discredit the Catholic mystical teaching, and

---

[145] Hart, 411.

[146] Hart, 416.

[147] DeArteaga, 65.

[148] Ibid.

this was best served by relying only on the five senses and reason as the ways to know truth.[149] That rationalism led us to a place where, too often, modern Christians and ministers tend to misunderstand what it means to believe. They tend to think that it means to believe in your intellect, whereas scripture teaches that we are to believe in all areas of the inner man.[150]

Now, when it comes to getting real, effective faith, there is one exception to the rule of "by hearing," and that would be the "gift of faith" in 1 Corinthians 12:9. Since this faith is a special and spontaneous work of the Holy Spirit, the regular principle does not apply. Describing such an experience, Smith Wigglesworth (a hero of faith preceding, and admired by, the leaders in the modern WOF movement) said, "Oh, of this wonderful faith of the Lord Jesus. Your faith comes to an end. How many times I've been to the place where I have had to tell the Lord, 'I have used all the faith I have,' and then He has placed His

---

[149] Ibid., 86.

[150] Ibid., 199.

own faith within me."[151] In other words, when one cannot believe, because God's will is not specifically revealed in Scripture, or a person has not had sufficient opportunity to build their faith, God can empower them by His Spirit with a faith that cannot doubt, the faith that achieves the required result. For example, since scripture does not generally promise the power to kill trees, Jesus must have been specifically led and empowered by the Spirit to do so in Mark chapter 11.

So, the Word of Faith movement teaches that, generally, God expects us to use the faith we have, the faith that comes from hearing the word of God. Furthermore, since God has revealed how to get faith, it is our responsibility to respond to that truth by applying ourselves to hear God's word and build our faith for what we desire or need from him.

This sense of spiritual responsibility can sometimes come as a shock to people outside the movement. Where some Christians view prayer as a wish that might come true and might

---

[151] King, 176.

not come true, the Word of Faith movement emphasizes that God meant what he said in his word, so if we come to him as he prescribed, we can fully expect him to do what he said. Conversely, we can also be sure that, if we neglect to learn what his word says, our prayer life will largely be an exercise in futility. Though God is compassionate toward the weak and unlearned, he does not reward laziness. He fully expects us to value truth enough to seek it, learn it, and grow up into Christ.

What Faith is

Now that we see what the Word of Faith teaches about how faith comes, we need to look at the movement's understanding of the distinct nature of faith. As he begins to explain this point, Hagin insists:

> we must understand that there are a number of kinds of faith. For example, everyone has a natural human faith, whether they are saved or unsaved. But in Hebrews 11:1, God is talking about a scriptural faith—a Bible faith. *Bible faith is believing with your heart.* There is a vast difference between believing with your heart, and just believing what your physical senses may tell you.[152] (emphasis added)

---

[152] Hagin, *Bible Faith...*, Location 297.

So, according to Hagin, the basic definition of Bible faith is "believing with your heart."

The contrast that he makes here between different kinds of faith is not new or unique to the Word of Faith movement. "Church father Cyril of Jerusalem, writing in the fourth century, described a natural faith that all men have while distinguishing this form of faith from that which is bestowed by Christ as a gift of grace."[153] While the world knows a natural faith based on natural evidence, the Bible reveals a spiritual faith based on divine revelation.

Interestingly, as he continues to clarify, Hagin first offers explanations of what faith is *not*. As in the quote above, he uses Hebrews 11:1 as a primary text: "Now faith is the assurance of things hoped for, the conviction of things not seen." He points out that, though faith and hope often work together, Bible faith is *not* hope. He explains that, where hope looks to the future, faith believes in the now.[154] He explains that...

> Faith says, "It is mine. I have it now." Hope says, "I'll get it sometime." But as long as you are in hope and not in faith, whatever it is you are desiring will never

---

[153] King, 145.

[154] Ibid., Location 633.

materialize—it will never come into being. But the moment you start believing and acting like God's Word is so, your faith will work for you.[155]

He also points out that, in Mark 11:24, the believing comes *before* the having. In Hebrews 11:1, that faith is the "conviction of things not seen." This means that "faith is *not* sight," but rather, precedes it.[156]

Hagin also notes that, since believing precedes seeing, faith is *not* knowing. Bible faith believes *before* it sees. To know something requires experiencing it with the physical senses, whereas faith takes God at his word before physical evidence is available.[157] Hagin points out that walking according to natural sight and knowledge is what we're used to in this life. However, if we already see something, then Bible faith is no longer necessary, because we know it. As Jesus said to Thomas, "Have you believed because you have seen me? Blessed are those who have not seen and yet have believed" (John 20:29).

---

[155] Ibid., Location 764.

[156] Ibid., Location 810.

[157] Ibid., Location 1813.

Coming around to the affirmative side, Hagin utilizes the KJV wording of Hebrews 11:1, "Now faith is the substance of things hoped for, the evidence of things not seen." He explains that faith is giving substance to your hope, adding visible evidence to your belief, before seeing what you asked for.[158]

He also takes the "now" of Hebrews 11:1 as part of the description, rather than a transitional word. He takes "now faith is..." to mean that faith believes something in the present, where hope focuses on sometime in the future. He asserts, "If it's not now, it's not faith."[159] Accordingly, believing what one has prayed for is done, now, rather than it will happen sometime in the future, is critical to operating in Bible faith.

Though it can be argued that Hagin makes a grammatical misstep here, the overarching principle regarding "believing now" fits with Jesus' teaching in Mark 11:23-24. In both verses, Jesus indicates that believing it's as good as done the moment one

---

[158] Ibid., Location 902.

[159] Ibid., Location 645.

speaks or prays is crucial to the effectiveness of faith. (Also, some would argue that emphasizing "now faith is" serves as an effective instructional device, helping the idea to stick in one's memory, even if it's not the exact grammatical meaning of this specific passage.)

Sticking with Jesus' own example of cursing the fig tree: When he cursed it, it seems that he believed it was as good as done in that moment – it was only the disciples who were surprised when they later saw the external evidence. Jesus was operating by faith, while they were still operating by sight. (Sadly, I see that many Christians today sit content to operate like the disciples, rather than pursuing to become like the master. They pray and then start looking for natural evidence to see if their prayer was answered, rather than resting on God's word and believing that it is done the moment they say "Amen.")

Hagin explains that shifting faith's timing was the final missing step in receiving his own healing. Though he had prayed many times and sincerely believed that God would heal him at some point, he didn't experience healing until the Lord helped him to realize that he had to shift his faith into the now. When he recognized that he needed to believe he was healed *now*, and to act on his faith before he saw a difference, he threw his paralyzed legs over the side of the bed. After he clung to the bedpost for several minutes, thanking God he was healed, the power of God hit him and gave him the strength to stand.[160]

While Word of Faith teaching mainly emphasizes the potential of biblical belief, it also emphasizes the negative potential of unbelief. Since humans have a free will, and can choose to believe, they are also capable of refusing to believe, which the Bible calls "unbelief." Hagin writes that "unbelief is taking sides against God's word."[161] Where acting in faith in God's word facilitates the reception of God's promises, unbelief has the opposite effect: It refuses God's promise and frustrates his grace.

As an example of the power of unbelief, Hagin points to Mark 6:5, "And he could do no mighty work there, except that he laid his hands on a few sick people and healed them." He explains

---

[160] Ibid., Location 930.

[161] Ibid., Location 1045.

how Jesus was unable to work the works that he had worked in other places because the people's refusal to believe on him kept Jesus' healing power from flowing as he desired.

By Grace through Faith

The interplay of the human and divine elements is critical to the Word of Faith doctrine. Word of Faith adherents recognize faith as essential to our entire walk with God. Faith enables us to receive what God has provided, both for this life and the next.[162] However, faith does not operate alone. For faith to receive, God must have given.

Ephesians 2:8-9 plays a key role in explaining God's part: "For by grace you have been saved through faith. And this is not your own doing; it is the gift of God, not a result of works, so that no one may boast." This verse represents both sides of the spiritual equation: On the one hand, God has initiated a relationship with us without any basis on our own previous merit – by grace. On the other hand, we must believe what he reveals to us about his provision to accept and experience it – through faith. These two

---

[162] Harrison, 28.

dynamics work together and result in our salvation. If either side failed, the equation would not work: If God had not initiated, there would be nothing to believe and receive. But even if God has initiated, his will remains unrealized if we don't believe and receive it (as in Mark 6:5, above).

For the Word of Faith movement, this is seen as the rule for how every blessing of God becomes realized in our lives – by grace, through faith. First, we need to learn what God has provided for us. Second, we need to exercise our faith to receive it.

Critical in the understanding of faith is the realization that God has decided that faith would be the acceptable means for receiving from him. In Genesis 15:6, we see how God reacted when Abraham responded to his promise: "And he believed the Lord, and he counted it to him as righteousness." God is pleased when we believe him, and he responds to faith because that's just who he is. In other words, faith counts for something because…God has indicated that faith is the response he desires and rewards. Faith works because God has determined it would.

Since faith is a human response to God's grace, real Bible faith can only come when grace is revealed. As Paul noted, "So faith comes from hearing, and hearing through the word of Christ" (Romans 10:17). Though some speak derogatively of the Word of Faith movement as the "name it and claim it" bunch, there is a boundary around what God has provided and what we can reach out for in faith. That boundary is his revealed will. Hagin himself lamented, "I do not understand how some people can go around spouting off things, endeavoring to believe, and calling it faith, when it is only presumption and folly."[163]

Sadly, this balance of grace and faith has often been neglected or ignored – both by those inside and outside the movement. This has caused some to take issue with the Word of Faith movement, seeing it as putting a burden on people, requiring them to try to believe for hard or unrealistic things. However, there is a huge difference between believing and *trying* to believe – between believing and *wanting* to believe. The difference lies in understanding the genuine nature of Bible faith, as we have been discussing.

---

[163] Kenneth E. Hagin, *What to do when Faith seems Weak and Victory Lost* (Tulsa: Kenneth Hagin Ministries, 1979), 25.

Let's look at how Paul discusses Abraham's faith in Romans chapter 4:

> 18 In hope he believed against hope, that he should become the father of many nations, as he had been told, "So shall your offspring be." 19 He did not weaken in faith when he considered his own body, which was as good as dead (since he was about a hundred years old), or when he considered the barrenness of Sarah's womb. 20 No unbelief made him waver concerning the promise of God, but he grew strong in his faith as he gave glory to God, 21 fully convinced that God was able to do what he had promised.

In Abraham's specific case, he and Sarah had been unable to have children and were well beyond the natural childbearing years. Conception was naturally impossible. Yet God had promised them a child. The reason that Abraham was able to respond positively to God's promise was that, as he considered the deadness of his own body and his wife's, he also considered God's character and ability. When he did, God's part won him over. Faith came through hearing God's word.

As verse 21 states, Abraham was "fully convinced." He was not trying to believe. He was not straddling the fence. Though he had a natural hope of no child, he was persuaded by God's promise and began to have a godly hope that triumphed over his negative, though normal and natural, expectation.

114

That aligns with the description/definition of faith in Hebrews 11:1, "Now faith is the assurance of things hoped for, the conviction of things not seen." The word "assurance" here is the Greek word ὑπόστασις *(hypostasis),* meaning steadiness, firmness, courage, resolution, confidence, firm trust, and/or assurance.[164] The word speaks of a state of confidence attained by being positioned under the covering of a resolute contract. In this sense, faith is a trust or rest in the covering. Faith does not create the covering but recognizes it and positions one under it.

Furthermore, the word "faith" itself, the Greek πίστις *(pistis),* refers to a conviction based on being persuaded of/by God.[165] This helps us to see that faith is not a matter of trying to believe or wanting to believe; it is a matter of having weighed the evidence and being fully persuaded of God's will and his ability to fulfill it.

Therefore, we should not first ask, "What can you believe?" We should ask, "What did God say?" God's *offer*

---

[164] Thayer's Greek Lexicon.

[165] Ibid.

necessarily precedes acceptance. One cannot sign an agreement that has not been prepared ahead of time. And this is foundational to Word of Faith teaching, even before Hagin's formulations. "Kenyon understood that the Bible was self-limiting, and one cannot ask in faith for those things which are not promised in scripture."[166] Going back even further, Charles Spurgeon insisted:

> A definite promise is what you want.... In due season a promise presents itself, which seems to have been made for the occasion; it fits exactly as a well-made key fits the lock for which it was prepared. Having found the identical word of the living God you hasten to plead it at the throne of grace...[167]

Furthermore, though critics often malign Hagin for his formulaic approach to teaching faith, it should be noted that the first step he taught for receiving answers to prayer was to "look for scriptures that promise you what you want from God."[168] He would

---

[166] DeArteaga, 223.

[167] King, 94.

[168] Every year at Winter Bible Seminar in Tulsa, Hagin would teach on prayer in the morning services, taking Ephesians 6:18-20 and John 15:7 as his texts, soon leading to this statement. The author was in these meetings yearly for nearly a decade.

inevitably follow this up with: "Notice I said scriptures, plural." He taught that you can't base your faith on a solitary scripture; you need to get "multiple witnesses," so your faith has firm ground upon which to stand.

Believing with the Heart

Another important aspect of faith that Hagin taught is that faith is of the heart. In Mark 11:23, Jesus said, "...does not doubt in his heart, but believes..." Paul also makes this specific point: "For with the heart one believes..." (Romans 10:10). Notice, it does not say to believe with the head, but with the heart. As previously noted, Hagin points out that "Many people want to know it first, and then believe it."[169] However, since faith is of the heart, or spirit, we have to train ourselves to prioritize faith over what we see or know. This aligns with Proverbs 3:5-6,

> Trust in the Lord with all your heart,
>   and do not lean on your own understanding.
> In all your ways acknowledge him,
>   and he will make straight your paths.

The distinction between heart and head helps us to overcome our difficulties in trying to understand or comprehend how God is

---

[169] Hagin, *Bible Faith...*, Location 399.

working or how our answer to prayer will arrive. As Mark Hankins, a contemporary faith teacher, says: "We often get into trouble trying to figure out '*how* and *when*.'"[170]

Though faith takes God at his word and is persuaded that what he said is true, walking by faith does not place the believer in God's place of calling all the shots. God is infinitely creative and seems to delight in doing things differently every time.

Now, this is not to say that people within the Word of Faith movement (or Christians in general) do not overreach and try to play God. Keith Moore, one of my instructors at Rhema Bible Training College, shared his own story of asking God for a car – a green Buick – by a certain date. Now that date was completely arbitrary, meaning he picked it independent of any direction or promise from God. When that particular date came and went, he was discouraged that his prayer wasn't answered – until the Holy Spirit reminded him that Scripture doesn't generally promise us things on a timeline. Learning that trying to give God a due date

---

[170] Mark Hankins, *Maximum Joy*, audio file of a sermon from 2007, in possession of the author.

is presumptive, he asked God to forgive him and picked up his faith again. After a further length of time, he received his answer to prayer.

Therefore, because so many aspects of life and God's working remain uncertain from our vantage point, Hagin often reminded his audience that "You can have doubt in your head and still have faith in your heart."[171] What's important is acting out of your heart, so your faith is working, rather than acting out of your head, and negating what God wants to do.

Just as Abraham didn't know exactly when conception would occur, how Sarah would be able to physically handle the pregnancy, or what day the baby would be born, we often do not know all the details. We can't know the end from the beginning. That's God's privilege. He just asks us to do what we *can* do – believe. That's what Abraham did, and God came through.

That said, "leaning not" does not mean "throwing away." Some have so elevated the spirit and denigrated the soul that they completely ignore sound-mindedness, emotional health,

---

[171] Hagin, *Bible Faith…*, 383.

intellectual rigor, or strength of will. While we lean on God through heart faith, our soul is intimately involved, which is why we must renew our minds to cooperate in the process. As Oden explains, faith "embraces in a balanced way the assent of the mind, the trust of the heart, and the decision of the will."[172]

Continuing with the example of Abraham: God changed his name to Abraham, which means "father of a multitude" (Gen. 17:5) *before* Isaac was born.[173] So Abraham walked around introducing himself as the father of a multitude, well before it was a visible reality. This leads us to our next point in Hagin's paradigm.

Turning Your Faith Loose

Just as James asserted that "faith by itself, if it does not have works, is dead" (2:17), the Word of Faith movement asserts that faith must be expressed to become effective. However, where James focused specifically on actions accompanying faith, Hagin and the movement following in his footsteps place equal or greater

---

[172] Oden, 603.

[173] ESV footnotes on Gen. 17:5 give the definitions of Abram as "exalted father," and Abraham as "father of a multitude."

120

attention on what faith *says*. Also, in my experience with Christians from other denominations, I have very often heard the obedience of faith discussed, as pictured in James. Therefore, since the Word of Faith movement focuses significantly more attention on the speaking part – hence the name of the movement – we will focus our discussion here on faith expressing itself in words.

In his teaching about "how to turn your faith loose," Hagin begins with Mark 11:23 and Romans 10:10 – "Truly, I say to you, whoever says to this mountain, 'Be taken up and thrown into the sea,' and does not doubt in his heart, but believes that what he says will come to pass, it will be done for him" (Mark 11:23). "For with the heart one believes and is justified, and with the mouth one confesses and is saved" (Romans 10:10). Since both verses discuss the efficacy of believing and speaking, Hagin notes that "believing plus speaking equals activated faith."[174]

Speaking what one believes, in Word of Faith teaching, is commonly referred to as "confession." Where the Christian church

---

[174] Ibid., Location 2927.

historically emphasizes the "confession" of sin, or "confession" of creeds, the Word of Faith movement generally emphasizes the role of "confession" in receiving everything that God has supplied.[175]

The logic follows the thought that, in Romans 10:10, salvation comes through believing and confessing. It is not enough to believe alone. One must make an expression of their belief for it to become effective. Here, Paul indicates that the confession of faith is sufficient action, a form of expression that God accepts. While other texts reveal that appropriate action must necessarily follow, the speaking is enough to initiate the working of the power of God.

As a further note that should be stressed in this scheme: The word "salvation" in Romans 10:10 is the Greek σωτηρίαν *(soterian),* which, in context, refers specifically to conversion – salvation from sin. It is the noun form of the root verb σῴζω *(sozo),* meaning "to save." However, the concept of salvation in scripture is much broader than just eternal security. As we see in

---

[175] King, 254.

other contexts, σῴζω *(sozo)* applies to further aspects of redemptive rescue.

For example, when Jesus heals the woman with the issue of blood in Mark 5, he tells her, "...your faith has made you well..." (v. 34). The Greek for "made...well" there is σέσωκέν *(sesoken),* also a form of the verb σῴζω *(sozo).* For this reason, English translations generally render the text as "made you well," though the NIV reads "has healed you." Additionally, a few read literally "saved you" (CSB, NAB, YLT...).

So, because Jesus uses the word "saved" to mean more than just conversion, Word of Faith teaching sees Romans 10:10 and Mark 11:23 as revealing the general spiritual principle that faith and words work together to receive saving grace in its various forms or applications. Hagin calls this combined operation of faith and words "confession unto..."[176]

Important in this discussion of confession is the definition of the word "confess," which Webster defines as: 1. To tell or make something known, 2. To acknowledge (sin) to God or a

---

[176] Hagin, *Bible Faith...*, Location 3495.

priest, 3. To declare faith in or adherence to, and 4. To give evidence of.[177] In all of these cases, the words spoken are an expression of, or in agreement with, something that is already true.

Similarly, Hagin defines confession in the following ways: "1. Confession is stating something we believe. 2. Confession is declaring something we know to be true. 3. Confession is proclaiming a truth we've accepted wholeheartedly."[178]

The Word of Faith movement understands that salvation is realized in the life of a person by believing and coming to agreement with the truth about Jesus. As Romans 10:9 states, "because, if you confess with your mouth that Jesus is Lord and believe in your heart that God raised him from the dead, you will be saved." The confession does not *make* Jesus Lord; it only acknowledges what is already true and applies it personally. Where Jesus is universally Lord, when confessed, he effectively becomes my Lord.

---

[177] Merriam Webster, "Confess," https://www.merriam-webster.com/dictionary/confess.

[178] Hagin, *Bible Faith...*, Location 3000.

It is by acknowledging that truth with one's mouth that one crosses over from darkness to light. It is when we speak in agreement with the Gospel that we activate, or connect to, the power already present in the Gospel, resulting in our salvation. It is in this way that the phrase, "confession brings possession" – both popular in the movement and infamous outside it – proves true.

Word of Faith teaching generally follows this line of thought, encouraging believers to discover and speak in line with God's revealed word. Hagin teaches:

> Our confession needs to center around these principal truths: 1. What God has done for us through Christ in His plan of salvation. 2. What God has done in us by the Word and the Holy Ghost in the new birth and the infilling of the Holy Ghost. 3. Who we are to God the Father in Christ Jesus. 4. What Jesus is presently doing for us at the right hand of the Father where He ever lives to make intercession for us. 5. What God can accomplish through us, or what His Word will accomplish through us as we proclaim it.[179]

Interestingly, though critics often focus only on Word of Faith people trying to *get* something for themselves through confession,

---

[179] Ibid., Location 3007.

the focus is generally on discovering what Scripture says is true and speaking in a way that agrees with God. In this way, confession is most about conforming one's thinking to a more biblical worldview. In other words, it's an instrument for renewing the mind. As God told Joshua as he prepared to assume command of Israel:

> "This Book of the Law shall not depart from your mouth, but you shall meditate on it day and night, so that you may be careful to do according to all that is written in it. For then you will make your way prosperous, and then you will have good success" (Joshua 1:8).

Keeping God's word in his mouth would keep it in Joshua's attention and thoughts, helping him to persist in walking fully according to God's Law and will.

Going back to Numbers 13, Word of Faith teaching also recognizes an important distinction between the reports of Caleb and Joshua and the other ten spies regarding the Promised Land. While Caleb and Joshua agreed with God, saying, "Let us go up at once and occupy it, for we are well able to overcome it" (v.30), the other ten brought what Scripture defines as a "bad report" (v.32). This report manifested more than an honest assessment of the challenges they faced; it demonstrated a lack of trust in God.

Their report expressed a negative judgment regarding God's intention and ability to give them the land. In the end, the people of Israel followed the ten in their response of unbelief (14:1), which resulted in God's judgment and 40 years of wandering in the wilderness.

Therefore, because Scripture defines the negative report in moral terms (as "bad," or "evil" in other translations, such as KJV, ASV…), and since it brought about painful consequences, the Word of Faith movement takes a generally resistive posture towards negativity, especially negative speaking. Negative speaking is seen as contradicting Scripture's testimony regarding God's promises, so adherents are encouraged to speak what God says about them and their situation. Because of this stance, confession in the Word of Faith movement is often described as "positive confession."

The use of the term can be justified as aligning with Scripture when rightly defined, understood, and applied. However, positive confession has often been seen by outsiders in negative terms – as emotional gamesmanship, American cultural cheerleading, or even manipulative speech policing. Sadly, people in the Word of Faith movement are human and do, for various reasons, fall into these errors at times, giving substance to the accusations. This explains Harrison's note, "This practice of speaking only in positive confessions is one of the most readily apparent, misunderstood, and derided elements in the Word of Faith system of beliefs and practices."[180] However, while some struggle to appropriately apply these scriptural truths concerning our words, we would be wise to avoid discarding the whole of the biblical teaching on the subject. As Paul prayed regarding love, we may need to pray regarding our speech:

> And it is my prayer that your love may abound more and more, with knowledge and all discernment, so that you may approve what is excellent, and so be pure and blameless for the day of Christ, filled with the fruit of righteousness that comes through Jesus Christ, to the glory and praise of God. (Philippians 1:9-11)

Just as Christians historically struggled to exercise their love regarding sacrifices offered to idols, mixed marriages, etc., we probably need to recognize we have a ways to go in our maturity

---

[180] Harrison, 10.

regarding our faith-filled conversation and how we encourage one another in it. However, that gap should not be used as grounds for capitulation, but rather, for a more thoughtful embracing of God's ideal.

The Power of Words

Now, a main reason that the Word of Faith movement makes such a big point of watching their confession is that they believe words are powerful. As previously noted, the Word of Faith teaching sees Genesis 1 as depicting humans created in the image of God to include a relatively high degree of similarity, including a spiritual nature. Following this line of thought, since one of God's first revealed characteristics is that he speaks and creates, Word of Faith teaching sees humans as speaking spirits whose words also (have the potential to) carry power. As Harrison notes, "The Faith Message teaches believers that...it is a spiritual law that the spoken word sets creative (or destructive) forces in motion."[181]

---

[181] Ibid.

There are many texts in Scripture that discuss the influence of words and the power of God's words. James 3 describes the tongue as a rudder (v.4), as a flame (v.6), etc. Proverbs is also full of insight about the tongue with many passages describing its potential to produce good or evil (i.e., 15:4, 15:28, 21:23…).

Addressing this, Hagin writes,

> If you talk about your trials, your difficulties, your lack of faith, your lack of money—your faith will shrivel and dry up. . .. If you confess sickness, it will develop sickness in your system. If you talk about your doubts and fears, they will grow and become stronger. If you confess your lack of finances, it will stop the money from coming in.[182]

Bowman takes issue with this idea, asserting that, "God's words are the most powerful things in the universe because he is God…, not because words in and of themselves are powerful."[183] King also points out that, where Smith Wigglesworth taught that God's word had creative force, some contemporary faith teachers seem

---

[182] Kenneth E. Hagin, *How to Write Your Own Ticket with God* (Tulsa: Kenneth Hagin Ministries, 1979), 10.

[183] Bowman, 200.

to cross the line and teach that man's words possess creative force.[184]

However, it seems that the Word of Faith approach has merit when properly understood – though that appears to require some clarification. Though human beings are not God, and therefore do not inherently possess creative power, Scripture does teach that spiritual power influences, cooperates with, and flows through our words. We have already mentioned that our confession activates the power of the Gospel to save us. That seems to align with the middle aspect (above), that our words "cooperate" with the power of God, so let's look at examples of the other two: How our words are spiritually influenced, and how they work as vessels of spiritual power.

First, if we look at James 3 and Acts 2, we see spiritual fires that motivate/influence speaking. James writes, "And the tongue is a fire, a world of unrighteousness. The tongue is set among our members, staining the whole body, setting on fire the entire course of life, and set on fire by hell" (v.6). Conversely,

---

[184] King, 164.

Luke writes, "And divided tongues as of fire appeared to them and rested on each one of them. And they were all filled with the Holy Spirit and began to speak in other tongues as the Spirit gave them utterance" (v.3-4). In both texts, we see spiritual "fire" that influences human speaking.

Regarding the spiritual potential, or impact of that speech: In James, it is the work of the devil unto destruction (cursing people – 3:9), and in Acts, it is the work of the Holy Spirit that ultimately results in 3,000 souls coming to salvation. In both cases, though one may insist that human speech does not inherently carry power, it does have the potential to carry the power of holy or evil spirits.

Paul echoes this in 1 Corinthians 14:4, explaining that "the one who prophesies builds up the church." Since Paul defines prophecy as human speech in the known language inspired by the Holy Spirit, leading to the spiritual edification of individual believers (v.3), it appears that Scripture *does* teach that words have power – or at least that words can carry spiritual power. This would also seem to be obvious when we consider Paul's exhortation in Ephesians 4:29, "Let no *corrupting talk* come out of your mouths, but only such as is good for building up, as fits the occasion, that it may *give grace* to those who hear."

Clearly, our speech has the power to work good or evil, and that is not only contractual/natural, or emotional/intellectual, but also spiritual. So, when Word of Faith teachers comment that "words have power," if it is understood as a summary expression of the above realities, then it seems to be firmly rooted in biblical truth.

Returning to the Genesis 1 image of God discussion, the functional view impacts the Word of Faith perspective on words as well. Since God created us to have dominion over the earth, as stewards of his delegated authority, and God speaks words of authority to express his dominion, Word of Faith teaching sees words as a way that we exercise our dominion from God. For example, Hagin writes that God instructed him not to pray for finances anymore. Since all the resources one needs are present on earth, and God gave humanity dominion over the earth, Hagin was told to "just claim what you want and what you need."[185]

---

[185] Hagin, *Bible Faith…*, Location 3262.

This authoritative speaking, rather than praying, is built on the contrast between Mark 11:23 and Mark 11:24. In verse 24, Jesus teaches his disciples to pray in faith, whereas in verse 23, he teaches them to command the mountain to move. When Jesus cursed the fig tree – upon which this instruction is based – he did not pray about the tree; he spoke to it. Since he is training his followers to do as he did, it follows that we can and should do what he instructed, to similar effect.

Critical here is Jesus mention that a person "not doubt in his heart, but believes that what he says will come to pass" (Mark 11:23). Since we know that biblical, heart faith only comes by hearing the word of God/Christ (Romans 10:17), Word of Faith teaching asserts that one cannot simply go around saying anything he or she wants and expect it to happen. One must have God's word on the subject.

Furthermore, the delegated dominion which humans are allowed to exercise is limited to the sphere of influence that God has allotted to them. Scripture is replete with descriptions of roles, responsibilities, and authority – whether of prophets, kings, and priests, or husbands, wives, masters, and servants. Each has a definite, yet limited sphere of authority and influence. At a most basic level, I am responsible for my response toward God, renewing my mind, and disciplining my body. No one can do that for me. I have the authority *and* responsibility. (This truth would free many pastors from condemnation, as they realize that they can teach their people, but their people own their choices.) And, just as I cannot sell my neighbor's house, because his name is on the title deed, I cannot exercise spiritual influence through biblical faith in areas where God has not placed me in charge.

That said, we read in scripture where Jesus has given us authority in his Name:

> You did not choose me, but I chose you and appointed you that you should go and bear fruit and that your fruit should abide, so that whatever you ask the Father in my name, he may give it to you. (John 15:16)

> And he said to them, "Go into all the world and proclaim the gospel to the whole creation. Whoever believes and is baptized will be saved, but whoever does not believe will be condemned. And these signs will accompany those who believe: in my name they will cast out demons; they will speak in new tongues; they will pick up serpents with their hands; and if they drink any deadly poison, it will not hurt them; they will lay their hands on the sick, and they will recover." (Mark 16:15-20)

These two verses demonstrate that Jesus has given us the use of his name as an expression of delegated authority to accomplish Kingdom purposes. We can use that name and subsequent authority for all the purposes he has prescribed. (Now, obviously, we don't "command" the Father when using Jesus' name in prayer, but we are praying in identification with Jesus, as though Jesus himself were asking.)

The problem is that Jesus uses generous terms to describe what he has delegated, saying "whatever you ask" in John 15, and giving us a whole list of signs in Mark 16, just to use these two examples. However, it seems people are more prone to limit what God wants to do in their lives than to embrace its glorious fullness.

And this makes sense when we consider that we have an enemy who is attempting to withstand the advance of the Kingdom (Matthew 16:18). To stop our advance, he works to hinder our grasp of our rights and abilities in Christ. So, though thousands of years have passed, and we now live in the age of abundant grace and the outpouring of the Holy Spirit, there are still far too many saints who hold to the Numbers 13 "bad report" view of themselves, seeing themselves merely as "grasshoppers."

Sadly, too many Christians are ignorant of the enemy's devices and allow him room to influence their speech. Though they may think that they are just speaking their mind, they are often making an evil report by saying things about themselves (and others) that are unbiblical. At best, they are frustrating the grace of God. At worst, they are agreeing with the enemy and spreading satanic corruption in their lives, families, churches, and communities. For this reason, I find that this teaching on the spiritual potential of our words is not only biblically valid, but vitally essential for the good of the Body of Christ and the advancement of the Kingdom of God.

Say it, Then See it

The application of confession, in the Word of Faith understanding, also provides practical guidance for the believer in their faith between the "Amen" and the "there it is." In other words, "confession" is speaking in agreement with God's promise of answered prayer before the answer becomes visible. For example, Hagin writes, "Make the confession that by His stripes you are healed. The disease and its symptoms may not leave your body at once, but as you hold fast to your confession, those symptoms will leave."[186]

Hagin uses Hebrews 4:14 as foundational here: "Since then we have a great high priest who has passed through the heavens, Jesus, the Son of God, let us hold fast our confession." And, returning to 2 Corinthians 4:13 "Since we have the same spirit of faith according to what has been written, "I believed, and so I spoke," we also believe, and so we also speak..." Both contexts refer to speaking what one believes, of agreeing with unseen truth that is based on revelation.

And, returning to Abraham as our model, in Romans 4, Paul presents him as our "father of faith":

> 16...the one who shares the faith of Abraham, who is the father of us all, 17 as it is written, "I have made you the father of many nations"—in the presence of the God in whom he believed, who gives life to the dead and calls into existence the things that do not exist. 18 In hope he believed against hope, that he should become the father of many nations, as he had been told, "So shall your offspring be." 19 He did not weaken in faith when he considered his own body, which was as good as dead (since he was about a hundred years old), or when he considered the barrenness of Sarah's womb. 20 No unbelief made him waver concerning the promise of God, but he grew strong in his

---

[186] Hagin, *Bible Faith...*, Location 5624.

faith as he gave glory to God, 21 fully convinced that God was able to do what he had promised.

In Abraham's specific situation, he had God's promise that he and Sarah would receive a son. Between the time that this was promised and the time when they conceived, Abraham had to continue to believe God, which involved both speaking and acting his faith. Concerning the acting part, he had to work on the natural side of conception, though he knew that he and Sarah's bodies were "dead." On the speaking side, God had changed his name to "father of a multitude" (Gen. 17:5), so he had to accept that name change and go around telling everyone he met: "Hi, I'm no longer the 'exalted father,' I'm the 'father of a multitude.'" At this point, strangers must have inevitably asked him, "Wow! How many kids do you have?" To which he had to reply, "Just one from my wife's maid right now, but God has promised us more."

Now, with Abraham's wealth, his servants and trading partners were most likely cautious to put on a good face in his presence. Behind his back, they may have been tempted to ask each other: "Has our master become senile? He takes good care of us, but he's become quite a dreamer!" Those who were not dependent on him must have raised objections to his face: "Why do you call yourself that…when you have no sons in your house?" Hopefully, since ancient Near Eastern naming conventions would have made this appear more normal in their eyes, many would have replied with a Godfearing and gracious, "May the Lord make it so."

I point this out because Scripture teaches us that people are just people – even our heroes of faith. If "Elijah was a man with a nature like ours" (James 5:17), then Abraham was too. He probably had to deal with questions – both from within his own mind and from those around him – on a daily basis. He was surely tempted to lay down his faith and give up. But he did not.

Neither did Sarah. We read that Abraham did not "waver concerning the promise of God, but he grew strong in his faith as he gave glory to God, fully convinced that God was able to do what he had promised" (Romans 4:20-21). However, Sarah also kept her faith in God's promise. Hebrews 11 tells us that "By faith Sarah herself received power to conceive, even when she was past the age, since she considered him faithful who had promised. Therefore from one man, and him as good as dead, were born descendants as many as the stars of heaven and as many as the innumerable grains of sand by the seashore" (vv. 11-12).

Regarding the timing of Sarah receiving strength, we don't have Scripture that says if she received strength the day God promised or at the point of conception. Knowing how God often works – as in the case of Naaman the leper dipping seven times (2 Kings 5), or Elijah praying for rain seven times (1 Kings 18) – he often allows us to take several tries of faith (feeling or seeing no change) before the manifestation of the promise becomes visible. Since God promised a child in one year, but pregnancy lasts 9 months, it is very possible that the faith couple tried to conceive for several months before the power of God was evident.

This is why the confession of faith is critical. It provides instruction for believing God between the promise, the prayer, and God's performance. As previously mentioned, God does not usually promise us a thing by a time (though he did with Isaac's birth). Therefore, in the in-between time, we are to speak in line with what we believe, not with how things appear. Our speaking and acting in faith keep us moving forward as we patiently await the fulfillment of God's word.

As a further example related to prayer, in Daniel 10 we see Daniel praying and fasting. On the 24th day, an angel appears to him:

> Then he said to me, "Fear not, Daniel, for from the first day that you set your heart to understand and humbled yourself before your God, your words have been heard, and I have come because of your words. The prince of the kingdom of Persia withstood me twenty-one days, but Michael, one of the chief princes, came to help me, for I was left there with the kings of Persia... (Daniel 10:12-13).

This serves as a rational foundation to believe what Jesus taught in Mark 11:24 – that we are to believe we receive *when* we pray. The angel tells Daniel that his words were heard "from the first day," but it took time for the angel to make the journey to bring him the answer. If the answers to Daniel's prayers were immediately sent but took some time to become evident, we can expect the same with our prayers. This demonstrates that faith is not a fantasy. Bible faith is based on evidence – just Scriptural, spiritual evidence rather than earthly, natural evidence. God does not ask us to believe a lie; he asks us to believe what is true, yet currently invisible to our physical eyes.

Of course, there are some major differences between the prayer of faith and Daniel's prayer. We do not know that Daniel was praying for something that he specifically knew God had promised; it may have been a more intercessory pleading and discussion with God. We do know that Jesus had not come, so Daniel was not able to pray with the authority of the name of Jesus, or to apply the teaching of Mark 11:24, because it had not yet been spoken. Today, we have some definite advantages. When we pray the prayer of faith based on a revealed promise of God, we can believe we have received "when we pray," not when we first see the result.

So, since we believe the answer is given when we pray, our speaking before we see it should align with God's word. As Hagin teaches, "Faith says, 'It is mine. I have it now.'"[187] And, conversely, "If you want to wait and possess your petition first, and then confess it, you're wrong. You've got the cart before the horse."[188]

---

[187] Hagin, *Bible Faith...*, Location 791.

[188] Hagin, *Bible Faith...*, Location 5514.

Now, it must also be noted that this only applies to the "prayer of faith" (as it is titled in James 5). As Paul explains in Ephesians 6:18-20, there are various types of prayer, suited to different purposes. The "prayer of faith" is a prayer that recognizes, reaches out, and receives a specific, clear, revealed promise of God. That's why James describes its operation to work as a standard rule or law: Sick? => elders pray the prayer of faith => healing.

That said, in other situations, prayer must work differently. For example, people outside the WOF movement often take issue with Hagin's assertion that at times it is "unscriptural to pray to God for healing using the words, 'If it be Thy will.'"[189] But his comment only applies when praying this specific prayer – the "prayer of faith." Since the prayer of faith has a specific biblical foundation – a revelation of the enduring word of God – it does not need to ask if a thing is God's will. Scripture has already revealed that it is.

---

[189] Ibid., Location 219.

There are many other contexts where we seek the will of God because it has not been specifically revealed – such as where to move, who to marry, etc. However, when we come to God for salvation, we must know that God has sent his Son because he desires to save us. And, as James indicates, healing is included as an element of our salvation for which we need no specific confirmation of the will of God.

.

SECTION 2: DEFENDING THE ORIGINS

Thoughts on Critique

As mentioned in the introduction, as the Word of Faith movement became more visible and influential, a variety of critical voices arose. Some of these have published works offering their critique, ranging from opinions that "the Word of Faith is heresy" to "the Word of Faith provides valuable insights, with some caveats." Here are a few notable examples, most of whom have already been quoted in this work:

- Charles Farah, *From the Pinnacle of the Temple (1979)*
- Dan R. McConnell, *A Different Gospel (1988)*
- Robert Bowman, *The Word-Faith Controversy (2001)*
- Hank Hanegraaff, *Christianity in Crisis (1993)*
- Gordon Fee, *The Disease of the Health & Wealth Gospels (1985)*

As mentioned in the introduction, there is an apostolic Gospel message for which we should contend, and it is right for believers to exercise discernment – especially when it comes to leaders, especially as it applies to their teaching and conduct. For this reason, now that we have examined the core teachings of faith and confession, it seems wise to examine the claims of critics for elements of validity and allow criticism to exercise a constructive influence, where possible.

Several critics point out that leaders in the WOF movement are prone to avoid critique, using a "touch not mine anointed" defense.[190] And while Scripture is clear that we should give honor where honor is due (Romans 13:7), and that elders who labor in preaching and teaching are worthy of double honor (1 Timothy 5:17), that does not place anyone above scrutiny. If anything, we must remember that teachers are warned that they will receive stricter judgment (James 3:1). So, though we should endeavor to preach the word of God (2 Timothy 4:1-2), and the word of God

---

[190] McConnell, 202.

is perfect (Psalm 19:7), we must remember that our individual doctrine is not.

That said, we must also beware of false motives and critical spirits that aim to squelch anything that God is doing. Just as the Pharisees in their day tried to stop Jesus because he did not fit within their theological (or more importantly, political) framework, people today still try to put the brakes on others who are outside their circle. Sadly, those we like to label "extreme" are often just willing to go a bit further than we are. Whether they are extreme or just more committed than we are is an important consideration.

I say this because not all critique is of the same quality, and therefore not equally valid. For example, as DeArteaga points out, "behind [Hanegraaff's] numerous citations and quotations lies a profound methodological error – the assumption that listing the worst errors of a movement is a truthful representation of that movement."[191] DeArteaga continues, arguing that "religious

---

[191] DeArteaga, 269.

movements generate both the extreme and the moderate examples."[192]

King notes, "While *some* of the criticisms of anti-faith writers have a legitimate base, one finishes reading many of the more derisive denunciations wondering if there is such a thing as a 'walk of faith.'"[193] Therefore, since we have established that there is a biblical walk of faith and God still requires and responds to faith today, we must be careful to ascertain the perspective of the respective critics and measure their words against Scripture. Some of them have tended to "throw the baby out with the bathwater." So, we want to glean what we can in a spirit of Christian unity, while avoiding the condemnation of Satan.

The Question of Origins

One of the primary concerns of the critics is the origin of the faith message. And, since our express purpose in this work is to contend for the original, apostolic faith, we must consider the

---

[192] Ibid., 270.

[193] King, 16.

roots of the movement and whether they do reflect a connection to apostolic Christian teaching.

Critics also express concern about the doctrinal approaches toward healing and prosperity held by the Word of Faith. However, this work has not allowed room for those topics to be covered, though I hope to do so in a follow-up book.

To examine the roots of the Word of Faith message, since we have already examined the aspect of its formation in the life of Hagin, through his own experience of healing, etc., we will continue tracking it backwards through previous generations of Christian teachers. We will begin with Kenyon and work our way back.

Kenyon's Influences

As previously noted, Kenyon preceded Hagin in many aspects of faith teaching. He taught things like, "Faith's confessions create realities," and, "We unconsciously go down to our level of confession." [194] Kenyon's teaching, its origin, and its prevalence in the modern Word of Faith movement are

---

[194] King, 253.

McConnell's primary concerns. He asserts that Kenyon's teaching had more in common with New Thought metaphysics than historical Christian orthodoxy, stating, "Kenyon taught the same doctrines of healing, positive confession, and prosperity that New Thought and Christian Science had been teaching for decades."[195] McConnell described how Kenyon attended a school of oratory where New Thought and Christian Science originated, and used similar verbiage in the presentation of his teaching. However, McIntyre points out that Kenyon…

> published tracts refuting the metaphysical cults quoting their own literature. He marshaled statements from their own writings and compared the statements with the gospel. Ironically he said they [the metaphysical leaders] presented 'another Jesus,' not the Jesus of Paul and John.[196]

Furthermore, Bowman does an excellent job of presenting Kenyon's main points of doctrine over against those of New Thought, demonstrating that "Kenyon's system appears to have little resemblance overall to New Thought."[197] Therefore,

---

[195] McConnell, 35.

[196] McIntyre, 131.

[197] Bowman, 46.

Bowman asserts that "We cannot classify his teaching as belonging in the metaphysical tradition."[198] King offers a further answer to McConnell's perspective, noting that "McConnell's error was in not recognizing the parallels and similarities between New Thought ...and Keswick/Higher Life teaching."[199]

In reading these works, it occurs to me that Kenyon may have used verbiage that people in the metaphysical camp would recognize because he had been around them while in college. Speaking to the trends of that era, Bowman notes, "Ironically, even as interest in miracles and mysticism was increasing, the general culture was highly enamored of science, and virtually all religious traditions were trying to express themselves in scientific terms."[200] So, just as Paul preached in Athens in terms that the Athenians would understand, Kenyon attempted to present the Gospel in a way that the metaphysical group and the culture of his day could readily and easily grasp. Confirming Kenyon's aim, McIntyre

---

[198] Ibid., 47.

[199] King, 65.

[200] Bowman, 81.

asserts that, though critics suggest that Kenyon's teaching demonstrated more cultic ideas in later years, it was actually in these years that he most directly and most often confronted metaphysical heresies.[201]

As I noted earlier, Kenyon was ordained a Baptist, identified himself as a Baptist, and maintained fellowship with Baptists his entire career, so his doctrinal foundation must have been closely related to theirs – and therefore, thoroughly orthodox. Though he officially left the Free Will Baptist denomination at one point, it was only because he disagreed with his local church board over financial matters.

It also deserves mention that though known for his message of faith, his last church was known for "his maturing emphasis on love."[202] Hagin's life and ministry have received similar attention, as he is known for faith, but he emphasized the love walk more and more in his later years. This is evidenced by the title of his 1994 book, *Love the Way to Victory*. Many who

---

[201] McIntyre, 170.

[202] Ibid., 127.

attended his funeral also report that faith was mentioned very little in comparison to the overwhelming testimony to his life of love toward others.

Returning to Kenyon's influences, Harrison echoes King's assertion that Kenyon was more influenced by the Higher Life movement.[203] Bowman, too, explains that "Kenyon's teaching was rooted in the pre-Pentecostal 'higher life' and healing or 'faith-cure' movements that paved the way for Pentecostalism."[204] Interestingly, DeArteaga points out that "Boston was the center for both the Faith-Cure movement and Christian Science."[205] Meaning, though Christian Science was present in Kenyon's environment, so was the Higher Life/Faith-Cure movement – for which Kenyon ultimately decided.

Classic Faith: Higher Life & Faith-Cure

I must admit that, before this research began, I had never heard of the Higher Life movement, though I was acquainted with

---

[203] Harrison, 53.

[204] Bowman, 59.

[205] DeArteaga, 213.

some of its most important figures. However, I have come to see that it provides a critical and categorical link to the teaching of faith in the past.

The holiness movement that began in the 1830s and preceded modern Pentecostalism was manifested in three streams: Wesleyan, Higher Life, and Keswick.[206] Higher Life teaching was based on holiness doctrines and taught that there are "three classes of human beings—the unsaved, the merely saved (who live lives of constant defeat), and the victorious Christian."[207] Confirming this movement's influence on the modern Word of Faith movement, one notes that Hagin uses the same structure and class descriptions in his teaching in *Growing up Spiritually*, though he uses the terms "the natural man," "the carnal man," and "spiritual man."[208]

The term "higher life" applies to the idea that one lives at a lower level – as merely saved – until one learns what God has

---

[206] King, 18.

[207] Dale H. Simmons, *E.W. Kenyon and the Postbellum Pursuit of Peace, Power, and Plenty* (Lanham, MD: Scarecrow Press, 1992), 86.

[208] Hagin, *Growing Up Spiritually*, note the table of contents.

provided in Christ and trains themselves to live as a "victorious Christian." Going from merely saved to a victorious Christian is understood as ascending to a higher level of life, so living this "higher life" in Christ becomes the goal. Though no longer presented in these exact terms, this idea is readily apparent as the same overall pursuit that much of the modern Word of Faith movement conveys.

Higher Life ministers preached a strong message of faith. A.B. Simpson (1843-1919), founder of the Christian & Missionary Alliance denomination, wrote:

> The blessings which God has to impart to us through the Lord Jesus Christ do not wait upon some sovereign act of his will, but are already granted, completed and prepared, and simply awaiting the contact of a believing hand to open all the channels of communication.[209]

Kenyon praised A.B. Simpson as having done more "than any other living man to spread the knowledge of the believer's privileges in Christ."[210]

---

[209] Quoted in King, 105.

[210] McIntyre, 82.

Another famous minister impacted by Higher Life was D.L. Moody (1837-1899), who taught that "believers should not just pray and believe for the promises of God, but claim them authoritatively."[211] Kenyon often referred to the group of men who most profoundly influenced his faith walk as "Moody's warriors."[212]

However, the man who most influenced that generation, and then Kenyon himself, was George Müller (1805-1898). George Müller is known to many as "the apostle of faith."[213] King explains that "Many of the contemporary faith principles regarding Mark 11:24, praying in faith for healing, claiming the promises of God for provision of needs and answers to prayer all came from the practical exercise of his faith."[214] As the founder and director of Ashley Down Orphanage, Müller was famous for not publishing what he needed, but just praying and trusting God

---

[211] King, 91.

[212] McIntyre, 105.

[213] King, 44.

[214] Ibid.

to supply. His resolute and effective walk of faith was inspirational to many – and was the specific influence that led Kenyon to make a break with his church board, because he wanted to run the church's finances as Müller had: solely on faith.[215]

There were many of that generation who taught a strong faith message, whom King calls the "classic faith leaders."[216] Charles Spurgeon (1834-1892), who many refer to as the "prince of preachers," was a close friend of Müller. "[Spurgeon's] devotional book *Faith's Checkbook* was based on the premise that the promises of God are appropriated by an act of faith, like endorsing in cashing a check, a common teaching in classic and contemporary faith movements."[217] He also related Deuteronomy 28 to Galatians 3:13 and believed that these two scriptures belong together.[218] And, similar to Hagin and the modern Word of Faith movement, classic faith teaching, exemplified by Spurgeon,

---

[215] McIntyre, 115.

[216] King, 108.

[217] King, 44.

[218] King, 92

Murray, and Simpson, "begins with a believer knowing his identity in Christ."[219]

A contemporary of Müller, whose impressive role often seems overlooked, is Methodist preacher Phoebe Palmer (1807-1874). Though Müller's feats of faith seem to gain more attention, possibly because of some historical gender bias in the Church, historian Charles White points out: "When the Pentecostal and Charismatic movement rose out of the holiness tradition, they took Phoebe Palmer's theology and added tongues to it."[220] Palmer's faith theology was best represented in her insistence on standing on "naked faith in a naked promise."[221] As a forerunner to Hagin and others, she taught that, "in the spiritual realm, the physical senses and emotions are to be subordinated to God's promises in the Word."[222]

---

[219] King, 87.

[220] Quoted in DeArteaga, 112.

[221] DeArteaga, 110.

[222] DeArteaga, 111.

Closely associated with Higher Life was Faith-Cure, which, as the name implies, focused on divine healing. Dr. Charles Cullis (1833-1892), an Episcopalian and medical doctor, is largely credited with bringing modern healing ministry to the United States. Bowman describes Cullis as "the single most important figure in the development of the divine healing movement in America."[223] After reading the works of Dorothea Trudel of Switzerland, in 1870, he began to offer healing prayers. "Within a short time, he had witnessed major healings through his prayers, including cancer, TB, and other diseases."[224] "Significantly, Dr. Cullis stated clearly that there was no conflict between faith healing and medical practice and that he constantly used both in his ministry."[225]

The Centuries Before

Luther stands tall among theologians for recovering the doctrine of salvation by grace through faith, bringing far-reaching

---

[223] Bowman, 60.

[224] Ibid., 115.

[225] Ibid., 116.

renewal to the Church. He also taught a strong faith message in general. Remarkably similar to modern faith teachers, he wrote, regarding James 5:15, "There is no doubt at all that if, at the present day, this kind of prayer were offered over the sick...as many as we desired would be healed. Nothing is impossible for Faith."[226]

Also, though we do not have the time to address in depth the "little gods" issue (which chafes several critics), it should be noted that Luther wrote: "This is what I have often said, that faith makes of us lords, and love makes of us servants. Indeed, by faith we become gods and partakers of the divine nature and name."[227]

DeArteaga points out that "The way Kenyon used revelation knowledge was bounded by scripture and, significantly, very similar to what Martin Luther originally proclaimed."[228] Luther also taught that "faith makes heirs."[229]

---

[226] Quoted in King, 32.

[227] Quoted in King, 31.

[228] DeArteaga, 237.

[229] Quoted in King, 31.

Going back even further, we continue to see Christians believing in the truth of faith and words working together. For example, monks in the Middle Ages understood that "in order to come alive, God's word had to take the living form of sound."[230]

We have already mentioned Bede in the 8th century and Chrysostom in the 4th. King notes regarding Theophilus in the 2nd century: "One of the earliest Church Fathers who stressed the importance of a life of faith, was Theophilus, a second century Bishop of Syrian Antioch. He laid down the axiom, 'Faith is the leading principle in all matters.'"[231]

Also in the 2nd century, Clement of Alexandria described faith as a power of God, similar to what contemporary faith teachers teach about faith as a force.[232] And, similar to Kenyon and Hagin, he "taught a distinction between knowledge by the senses and knowledge by faith."[233]

---

[230] King, 27.

[231] King, 25.

[232] King, 26.

[233] King, 25.

Having reached the 2nd century, we can go back no further. That takes us to the witness of the first century, which is the Scriptures themselves, which we have already explored in detail.

CONCLUSION

So, having explored the origins of faith teaching through the centuries, and seeing some rather surprising similarities to modern Word of Faith teaching throughout the ages, it seems clear that the critics' concerns regarding the origin of the Word of Faith movement are largely unfounded. Especially when we examine the teaching of the Higher Life movement that predates the Pentecostals, it seems to be sufficiently substantiated that the modern Word of Faith movement is a contemporary, unique, and generally orthodox expression of the Christian faith.

Furthermore, as we have examined the doctrinal core of the movement, defined as that which was taught by Hagin, we have identified the essential center of the Word of Faith movement. As we have explored what the movement teaches about the renewed nature of believers and the essential operation of words and faith, we have seen that these views are rooted in biblical truth and modeled in Scripture – both in the Old and New Testaments.

Now, that is not to say that issues do not remain, which should be highlighted and further discussed. There remains substantial confusion surrounding other beliefs and practices that deserve attention.

This thesis is the beginning of my conversation with the academic community and, hopefully, the Word of Faith community about where the movement stands and should be headed. The interest for this discussion initially arose from several side thoughts and mentions I discovered in academic materials during my M.Div. journey. Pursuing the study further, as time and topical focus allowed, I uncovered views of the movement that were both illuminating and disturbing.

On the one hand, I became painfully aware of the breadth of weirdness associated with our movement in the minds of scholars and Christians in general. And, not surprisingly, I found myself agreeing with some of the accusations. The failings and doctrinal errors they describe are so prevalent that they caused me to generally swear off Christian TV well over a decade ago. I saw myself in the description of Bowman, who shared: "My own experience of talking to people in the word-faith movement is that many, if not most, of them do not believe the heretical, and near-heretical ideas espoused by [some of] the leaders."[234]

This also led to the other side of my discovery: Many of the issues the critics voiced were related to things that I did not associate with the core of our movement's message. In fact, many of their biggest concerns echoed those I have heard voiced over the years by Kenneth E. Hagin and his son and successor, Kenneth W. Hagin, Jr. Other concerns appeared to illuminate areas that require clarification in terms that outsiders can better understand. Taking these things to mind, I realized that behind the terminology remains a core of doctrine that the Word of Faith carries that can be a helpful encouragement to others in the Body of Christ.

My hope is that I have been able to contribute to a more thorough definition of some of the basic tenets of Word of Faith

---

[234] Bowman, 228.

theology. Though I have not been able to touch on all the important topics or burning issues, I have used the little space I have to discuss the core of it all, faith and words, while trying to cover some common arguments and misunderstandings along the way.

I hope I will be able to continue this work in book form. This will allow me to cover the movement's understanding of healing and prosperity, which are huge pillars of faith and practice. I also have a lot to say about the "JDS" – Jesus died spiritually – discussion, about which many, both inside and outside of our movement, have very strong feelings and views. (It is hard to believe that I have invested so many hours and conversations in that one issue and couldn't fit it in here!) I realized I have also run out of space to touch on the "faith of God" language and other terminology issues, and these will be on my list for the next work.

That said, I have tried to present a biblical case for the basis of the life of faith. Since salvation and all the blessings of God are received "by grace through faith," we are never going to grow beyond our ability to use our faith as God both designed and requires. Where there are extremes, excesses, or errors, we must persist in our pursuit of what is good and true. As A.B. Simpson noted, "the best remedy for the abuse of anything is its wise and proper use."[235] So we don't want to run away from a life of radical faith in God. If we really care about the faith of the Church, we will double down on it.

The classic faith movement of the 19th century was an interdenominational and international movement that included people with a variety of theological perspectives, including Presbyterian, Baptist, Methodist, Quaker, Brethren, Dutch Reformed, and many more.[236] My hope would be that the teaching of the Word of Faith movement would continue to be clarified, refined, and communicated, so it can be an even greater encouragement to other movements, rather than increasingly walling itself off into a corner.

One of the European leaders of Rhema shared with me recently that they had been able to have fruitful discussions with the board of the Evangelical Alliance in their city. After dialogue over the board's various questions, the board was able to recognize

---

[235] King, 16.

[236] King, 24.

their church's doctrine as orthodox and accept them into that association. I hope this paper serves to assist such dialogue in other arenas and facilitate greater unity in the Body of Christ.

The Church worldwide still needs faith, because we still desperately need the miraculous power of God. As Theodore Christlieb, professor of Bonn University, wrote, "It is the want of faith in our age which is the greatest hindrance to the stronger and more marked appearance of the miraculous power which is working here and there in quiet concealment."[237] So, for those who long to see God move in their lives, families, churches, and nations, let us not lose heart, but press in to ever more contend for faith – and live by it!

---

[237] King, 78.

BIBLIOGRAPHY

Bowman, Jr., Robert M. *The Word-Faith Controversy*. Grand Rapids: Baker Books, 2001.

De Arteaga, William L. *Quenching the Spirit : Examining Centuries of Opposition to the Moving of the Holy Spirit*. Lake Mary, Fla: Creation House, 1992.

Got Questions. "What is Verbal Plenary Inspiration?" https://www.gotquestions.org/verbal-plenary-inspiration.html.

Hagin, Kenneth E. *Bible Faith Study Course, Kindle Edition*. Tulsa: Kenneth Hagin Ministries,1991.

_____. *Foundations for Faith*. Tulsa: Kenneth Hagin Ministries, 1998.

_____. *Growing up Spiritually*. Tulsa: Kenneth Hagin Ministries, 1976.

_____. *How to Write Your Own Ticket with God*. Tulsa: Kenneth Hagin Ministries, 1979.

_____. *How You Can Be Led by the Spirit of God*. Tulsa: Kenneth Hagin Ministries, 1978.

_____. Kenneth E. Hagin, *Right and Wrong Thinking*. Tulsa: Kenneth Hagin Ministries, 1966.

_____. *The Name of Jesus*. Tulsa: Kenneth Hagin Ministries, 1979.

_____. *The New Birth*. Tulsa: Kenneth Hagin Ministries, 1975.

_____. *What to do when Faith seems Weak and Victory Lost.* Tulsa: Kenneth Hagin Ministries, 1979.

Hankins, Mark. "Maximum Joy." Sermon audio, 2007, in possession of the author.

Harrison, Milmon Ferdinand. "'Name It and Claim It!': The Word of Faith Movement, the 'Faith Message', and the Social Construction of Doctrinal Meaning," 2001.

_____. "Word of Faith Movement." Encyclopedia.com. https://www.encyclopedia.com/religion/legal-and-political-magazines/word-faith-movement.

Hart, Larry D. *Truth Aflame.* Grand Rapids: Thomas Nelson, 1999.

Horvath, James Alexander. "Assessing the Need for Systematic Theology in the Curriculum of Charismatic /Word of Faith Bible Institutes and Colleges." ProQuest Dissertations & Theses, 2002.

Hubbard, Moyer V. *New Creation in Paul's Letters and Thought.* Cambridge: Cambridge University Press, 2002.

Kenneth Copeland Ministries. "About Us." https://www.kcm.org/about-us-0.

_____. "Kenneth Copeland Bible College Coming Fall 2018." July 10, 2017. https://blog.kcm.org/kenneth-copeland-bible-college-coming-fall-2018/.

Kenneth Hagin Ministries. "History of the Ministry." https://www.rhema.org/index.php?option=com_content&

view=article&id=9:history-of-the-
ministry&Itemid=132&showall=1&limitstart=.

_____. "What We Believe."
https://www.rhema.org/index.php?option=com_content&
view=
article&id=5&Itemid=138.

King, Paul L. *Only Believe*. Tulsa: Word & Spirit Press, 2008.

McConnell, D. R. *A Different Gospel: A Historical and Biblical
Analysis of the Modern Faith Movement*. Peabody, Mass:
Hendrickson Publishers, 1988.

McIntyre, Joe. *E.W. Kenyon and His Message of Faith: The True
Story*. Bothell, WA: Empowering Grace Ministries, 2010.

Merriam Webster. "Confess." https://www.merriam-
webster.com/dictionary/confess.

Nelson University. "The Life and Legacy of P.C. Nelson."
https://nelson.edu/pc-nelson-bio/.

Oden, Thomas C. *Classic Christianity*. New York:
HarperCollins, 1992.

Olsen, Ted. "Weblog: Kenneth Hagin, 'Word of Faith' Preacher,
Dies at 86." Christianity Today. September 1, 2003.
https://www.christianitytoday.com/ct/2003/septemberweb
-only/9-22-11.0.html.

Olson, Roger E. *The Mosaic of Christian Belief*. Downers Grove:
InterVarsity Press, 2016.

Perriman, Andrew. *Faith, Health & Prosperity*. Waynesboro,
GA: Paternoster, 2003.

Sherman, Bill. "BRIEF: Weekend conference to critique Word of Faith movement." Tribune Content Agency. July 7, 2012. https://go.openathens.net/redirector/regent.edu?url=https://www.proquest.com/wirefeeds/brief-weekend-conference-critique-word-faith/docview/1023910594/se-2?accountid=13479.

Simmons, Dale H. *E.W. Kenyon and the Postbellum Pursuit of Peace, Power, and Plenty.* Lanham, MD: Scarecrow Press, 1992.

The Azusa Street Revival. "F.F. Bosworth." https://www.azusastreet.org/Participant_Bosworth_F_F.htm.

Treier, Daniel J. *Introducing Evangelical Theology.* Grand Rapids: Baker Academic, 2019.

Made in the USA
Coppell, TX
24 April 2026

76461603R00101